Hobnail Boots on Tiny Hearts

by

Anna Barton

First published 2024

ISBN 978-1-9997082-4-5

Typeset, printed and bound in Poland.

This book is dedicated to
Our matchless Lord and Saviour Jesus Christ,
who makes all things new!

Acknowledgements:

To Karen, Trish and Dan for all of your diligent reading,
helpful suggestions and corrections.
So grateful

Contents

Introduction

I don't really remember much from my childhood and most of the memories I do have are not too pleasant but one early memory stays with me. It's probably the earliest memory I have. It's probably one of the best.

It is summer, I think, because there is a sunlit backdrop to the scene and midges are annoyingly buzzing around my face. We're walking along a leafy path near trees and shrubs. I say 'we' because I am fairly sure both my parents are with me. Actually, I should say that they are walking but I am being pushed in a pushchair and my curly blonde hair is blowing and bouncing around my laughing face. Maybe I am around two or a little older.

The fact that I am laughing and with both of them is significant enough but what is most significant is that it is the only happy memory I have from those early years. My only other happy childhood memory involving either parent will be at 10 when I came bottom of the class (a devastating blow for a bright child blighted by myopia and therefore unable to read the exam questions on the blackboard). I was so upset that mum gave me a hug; this act of comforting was the only physical affection I ever remember receiving from her as a child.

Much later I ask my mother where we had been going on that sunny, midge-filled day, and she, as usual, tells me some bitter tale about my erstwhile father. Of lies and disappointment; house viewings that never happened, house keys that mysteriously never appeared. Normality returns and that one positive glimpse of infancy is gone and forever tainted. In my teens I find a picture of me somewhere – two years old or so – playing in the garden and again there is a happy face with golden curls and laughter. I don't remember any of these other times, if they existed, but I now understand that trauma and pain are much more indelibly imprinted on the mind and heart of a child, obscuring so much that may have been good. Very recently though I found the picture of that sunny day and my walk with both parents. It was in my mum's house when we cleared it and I wonder if this is what I have really remembered all these years rather than the event itself. It does not matter – I now know without any doubts that it happened. There was a tiny but definite oasis of love which I once shared with both of my parents.

So, what of the rest? It has taken me more than 35 years to write down this story; I know this because I recently found scrappy notes which I had hastily scribbled when my children were tiny, filed away safely then lost. Notes which, once discovered, inevitably led me back to the difficult task of looking back on my life to recount the events, but more importantly their effects. I know now that it is a story which needs to be told. A story of pain. A story of control and deception. But more than all that, a story of hope. And this is why it needs to be told – to give hope to the many whose lives are not their own to live and who are not free to be the people they were created to be. This story is for you.

1. In the Beginning

In the early 1950s, Lancashire – in fact much of the North of England – was still shrouded in the economic and social legacies of the industrial revolution. Leigh, then a small bleak town about halfway between Manchester and Liverpool, had yet to emerge from the smog and dust of the age which had spawned it. Originally the cottage industry produced cotton – the damp air was eminently suitable – but huge mills took over in the 19th century and advantage was taken of the coal seams beneath. This industrialisation resulted in great wealth for some, hard labour for many and the pollution which nearly rubbed out my life in infancy and blighted my health throughout childhood. Smog was so bad in London at that time thousands died and they were named 'pea-soupers'. In Leigh you couldn't see your hand in front of your face in the worst winter fogs and I regularly had to wear a smog mask for my walk to and from school. In 1952, a year after I was born 12,000 died in London alone during or following the worst of these 'pea-soupers'. Only after the Clean Air Act in 1956, which introduced smokeless zones for domestic fuel burning and forced factories and mines to clean up the noxious pollutants they pumped into the air we all had to breathe, did things improve.

Born within a mile of the towering cotton mill where my mother was to work for so many years, I only just survived the Asian flu which swept through England when I was two. Perhaps this (and the air quality) was the reason that I suffered from asthma throughout my childhood – or perhaps it was the fear which gripped me almost every waking minute.

During her pregnancy with me my mum had been living in married quarters in Plymouth whilst my dad was on tour in the Far East. He was in the Royal Navy during a time when these tours of duty could last up to a year. At some point towards the end of the pregnancy Mum returned to live with her mother, my nana, in the North. When in my teens, I asked her why she would come and live with a woman who so obviously detested her and my father. She said there was no choice. Once more I was to hear a tale of bitter disillusionment with a husband who failed to provide for his pregnant wife; a story of near destitution which drove her to desperate measures out of sheer necessity.

These two women were to form the backdrop of my early years, their mutual hatred and contempt the emotional framework which helped to form my worldview and character. Together these two formidable, unhappy, twisted women became the substitute for parents who were to bring me up for the next 15 years. The fact that I survived is in itself a remarkable testimony to the Grace of God and the will of the human spirit to survive. The fact that I spent many occasions alone during these years planning how I could escape, including in my most despairing moments dark and violent thoughts which filled me with terror and shame for years afterwards. This stark evidence of the darkness that existed in my own young heart was later to form the basis of self-hatred as I turned this anger and frustration inwards, onto myself.

Nana

My grandmother, Josie McGuire, was a relic of the Victorian era. Born in 1900 she had grown up in an age when most women had little or no power or influence outside the home and therefore were intent on steering the domestic ship as tightly as possible. In some Northern women this meant extremely tightly indeed with husbands subjugated and children squashed. I never met either of my grandfathers but from all accounts my mother's father was treated with little respect or consideration by his wife. He killed himself when my mother was 19 and she was convinced that this was largely due to my grandmother's treatment of him (that is when she wasn't as equally convinced that he was murdered for his money belt). My paternal grandfather was a distant, shadowy figure I never met who, by my mother's assessment, was a violent bully who apparently beat my father mercilessly as a youngster. His wife was never, ever mentioned in our house, so Mrs McGuire was the only grandparent I would ever know. Even now this makes me shudder.

I was effectively reared by this woman while my mother was at work during my early years. A small, rotund woman by her mid-fifties, she wore horn-rimmed glasses and never went out without a hat securely anchored to her head by huge hatpins. She rarely smiled and was always at war with Mum. At home she was as nasty as she was mean. Unless of course we had visitors. These would be shown into the 'front room', a room kept only for this purpose and Christmas, where she would be charm itself both to them and to us. This transformation was so complete that I do wonder if she may have been inhabited by dual personalities. Once the visit was over she once more became her usual unpleasant self.

She was known to me as Nana, a term which I always associated with horrible, unhappy and quite frankly disturbing memories. When my first grandchild was born my daughter said we should call me Nana and thereby redeem the name, as I would be a nice Nana. Reluctantly I agreed to this and I have miraculously seen the name lose its horror. The person of my grandmother however has not.

As a very young child I soon became aware that children were to be 'seen and not heard'. This maxim was my grandmother's mantra for every situation where my presence might have intruded into her life or interfered with her will. This was in almost every situation. When my mother left for work in the morning I was left in her 'care'. I use the word loosely as this was probably one of the least caring environments I could have imagined for a young child.

Mum's hours were long and she would leave around 8.00am and not return until around 6.00pm. This time was my grandmother's domain and without fail she would make my life a misery.

I am not sure she positively hated me – that was an emotion and I am not sure she was capable of emotion – but her cruelty was not incidental or accidental and at times it was truly malevolent. I believed for many years that she hated my mother and that maybe influenced her treatment of me, but now I think she just took pleasure in cruelty. One instance which stands out even amongst the rest was the doctor's visit and was so typical of her actions and attitudes.

The Asian flu epidemic of the early 1950s had left its mark in my lungs, the dirty air surrounding us in my pre-school days adding to this. Asthma was a frightening and less understood condition then and there was little treatment. Inhalers did not exist and when an attack was bad coal-tar burners were the only things which brought any kind of relief. Bedrooms were unheated and winters a real danger. Vic vapour rub and Lucozade brought comfort but, in truth, nothing but rest and keeping calm helped.

At the beginning of the 20th century asthma was seen as a psychosomatic disease – an approach that probably undermined any medical breakthroughs at the time. During the 1930s to 1950s asthma was known as one of the *holy seven* psychosomatic illnesses.

Asthma was described as psychological, with treatment often involving, as its primary component, psychoanalysis and other 'talking cures'. A child's wheeze was seen as a suppressed cry for his or her mother. Psychoanalysts thought that patients with asthma should be treated for depression. This psychiatric theory was eventually refuted and asthma became known as a physical condition. However, there is no doubt in my mind that the condition is made worse by fear and depression – both of which were my childhood companions.

Asthma, as an inflammatory disease, was not recognized until the 1960s when anti-inflammatory medications started being used. Therefore, during my childhood asthma was still seen as something entirely in the mind of the sufferer. Perhaps this is a mitigating factor for what follows.

I am not sure of my age but I was probably around four or five. My mother was at work of course – employers were not sympathetic towards female employees taking time off for sick children. My condition had worsened during the early hours – 3.00 or 4.00am was always the worst time for those struggling to breathe after a bout of bronchitis. It was probably winter as I regularly spent long periods of time around Christmas in bed ill. I had not yet been diagnosed as allergic to house dust mites, that came much later, but I knew that dust would make me wheeze, cough and fight to breathe. Whatever the medical profession thought, there was a very real possibility that I might lose that fight. It must have been bad because the doctor had been called for and was to make a house call; this was a last resort, reserved for serious conditions then even more so than it is now.

My grandmother rarely cleaned upstairs, she seemed to live in the kitchen when she was not watching television in the middle room next to it. Cleaning was left to my mother at the weekends but the doctor was coming and therefore the house – especially the bedroom I shared with my mother – had to be spick and span. Doctors shared a level of status and power with the gentry and the bosses (just a little below deities) so we were prepared almost as if a visit of a minor Royal was due. It is the only time I ever saw her clean a window and the dust flew around the room almost as rapidly as she did.

Of course, this had a devastating effect on me and my little lungs and about halfway through this whirlwind dear Nana noticed that I was wheezing loudly and gasping for breath. I know now of course that asthma is partly physical and partly psychological and there is little doubt that the fear of not being able to take a breath made the experience worse still. Wild-eyed and terrified I probably looked alarming as I grasped the bedclothes and strained to breathe. To my grandmother, however, I seemingly looked comical. She would always joke when I experienced the hacking cough that accompanied bronchitis that 'It isn't the cough that you're coughing – it's the coffin they carry you off in...' and I must admit that as I got older I realised that was quite funny, in an odd way. However, as a young child struggling for oxygen it never seemed that amusing. What happened next though has stayed with me ever since and now that I am a grandparent of six adorable children who I love to distraction it is totally inexplicable how any sane person could behave in this way. That assumes that she was sane...

My Nana looked down from her furious window polishing and began to laugh, really laugh, not just a nervous giggle or slight gasp of amusement. She actually found my distress funny. 'Oh!' she cried, between giggles, 'you think you're going to die, don't you?' The fact was that this young child struggling to breathe probably did think that.

Then the doctor arrived and I remember nothing else of the visit, but as doctors terrified me throughout my childhood and well into my adult years, I was possibly catatonic by this time. Funny, that fear of doctors. It was not just a slight nervousness. I was terrified. I was frightened of many things actually, really ruled by fear for many years. Doctors however held a special terror for me until I was in my thirties. During a prayer time with some dear Anglican friends in Harrogate not long after I was saved, Jesus set me free from this fear and showed me the root of it.

Once more I think I can trace this back to my grandmother and I wonder if she used the same method to control her children. My recollection during that prayer time in Harrogate was of both Nana and my mother threatening me, but Mum says she never did this. Of course, she has said this about many things I now know to be true.

As a young child several methods were employed to keep me quiet and subdued. The use of physical violence was frequent, unpredictable and never spoken of. My mother used force to send me crashing across the room if I got in her way or caught her in a bad mood. This was followed by a complete reversal of attitude which usually involved her making me food, probably chips, in a sunny and pleasant mood as sudden and unexpected as the violence. I often wonder if my later weight problems stemmed from these feasts. I also often wonder if her bi-polar had ever been diagnosed whether my life would have been quite different.

Josie McGuire's methods were quite different and much more effective. She ruled through fear and a special kind of manipulation so favoured by her kind of woman. Her emotional control was complete and laid the foundations for all of my relationships for many years.

Her most effective threat was 'The Doctor'. As I said earlier, doctors were greatly respected and revered; alongside the priest they held much power over ordinary folk. The priest could throw you out of the Roman Catholic Church (as he had my mum when she married my dad) and the doctor could have you 'taken away'. Men in white coats may have been the subject of stand-up comedy in the late 20th century but in the 1950s they were a very real threat. And this was Nana's strategy. If I cried or got upset about their treatment of me, if I had a childish tantrum or wailed inconsolably, I was told that the doctor would be sent for to see what 'he could do with me'.

This was a very real threat to my little mind because only a few years earlier when I was two my baby teeth had all produced abscesses and the doctor had been sent for. Actually two men in suits came and held me down on the dining room table while a huge black mask was held over my mouth. The gas was to put me to sleep while all my baby teeth were taken out, but the trauma of that day made the thought of the doctor coming to sort me out terrifying. It also left me scared to death of dentists.

Although this threat to 'see what the doctor would do' was never carried out, for the rest of my life, until relatively recently, I was sure that I would one day lose control of my mind altogether and have to be taken away to the asylum. For many years I would not seek medical help for physical illnesses unless it was desperately needed and I was unwilling to go to the doctor with my many emotional and psychological problems under any circumstances. I was thoroughly convinced that I would be locked away forever; this belief stayed in my subconscious mind for most of my life.

Nana had other, more practical ways, of keeping me in my place. One of them was shutting me away somewhere. Initially I think this was under the kitchen sink. I say think because the memory is very vague, probably because I was very small then. But I do have a concrete sense of being frightened of running water. Whether this is because of the cupboard or because of Nana's method of rinsing my hair (holding my head under the tap while I spluttered and gasped for air – she seemed to like that scenario) I can't be sure. Waterboarding scenes in films seem unnervingly familiar. One thing I am sure of though is the cupboard under the stairs. Even as I write this I am aware of the fear and stress of this particular scene in the mind of that vulnerable little girl.

Picture a pre-school child – a pretty little thing with blonde, beautifully curly hair, still-trusting heart … if slightly dented by absent daddy and dodgy carers.

I don't know what I had done wrong, but it seems to me I am always crying inconsolably in this scene. I am always unhappy and upset before she shuts me in the cupboard. Maybe I was naughty and having a tantrum or maybe I wanted my mummy. Maybe it was just the unreasonable but quite normal behaviour of a two- or three-year-old. In any event she just wanted me to shut up; children were to be seen and not heard, remember, and if I was not going to be quiet then I was not going to be seen.

The cupboard under the stairs was typical of its kind in late Victorian terraced houses. The sloping ceiling began at the door about the same height as the door and went down to floor level at the far end. It was small and dark and lined with shelves along the left side. It was used for storage and in earlier times would house the cold slab which served to keep food cool before fridges were available. There was a light switch just inside the door but it was far too high for my little fingers to reach and when she grabbed me and pushed me in, locking the door behind me, I was plunged into total darkness. There was a small, red, three-legged stool in there which gave me the necessary height but if, as often happened, I could not find it in the darkened pantry I would quickly become hysterical.

The screams echo still in my head but they are not my screams now. They are the screams of this small, defenceless child who I cannot reach, as if it is happening to someone else. This is common in many of my childhood memories now. Remembered but not stored in my psyche. They are my memories but they no longer belong to me or hold any power over me. For this and many other mercies I am eternally grateful to my loving Heavenly Father.

Back in that understairs larder the hysteria gave way eventually to a kind of listless waking coma. I became quiet and submissive and no trouble at all. At this point the door would be opened and I was allowed out. Eventually after this treatment had been perfected the Pavlovian result was complete. My training was perfected; at home I became a total introvert. Unable to express my emotions and not allowed to show any negative feelings, I withdrew into myself more and more. My real life began when I was old enough to go to school, the only place where I could express myself, and I loved it there. At home I lived in a kind of fantasy world and had no sense of loving or being loved by mother or grandmother. Many times, if I even looked downcast, I was told to 'straighten your face or I'll straighten it for you' by one of them. I knew what kind of treatment would follow if I disobeyed and would plaster a smile on my face for the rest of the day. Being miserable was taboo and smiling the rule. It became easy for me to perform in any given situation and probably led to my desire to act when I was a young person. After all, I was acting my whole life. We all learn to wear masks, some of us at an early age, in order to survive in this world. Cruelty from the school bully, hatred of our skin colour or the fact that we are different in some way, makes us all pretend so that we can be accepted and loved. In the end we all want this and I especially wanted it from those who were meant to love and nurture me throughout my formative years. Actually, I would have settled for just feeling safe.

Even the infrequent visits from my father when I was little were to be a performance – from an early age I was instructed to run into this stranger's arms and give him a hug. He terrified me, reminding me of the convict in the black and white film version of *Great Expectations* and I cringed in his grasp. Fortunately, his visits were rare and stopped altogether when I was quite young, until I reached late teens.

My Dad

This is quite difficult for me as I know so little of my father. He was born in the 1920s and died sixty-odd years later and I can fill little of the years in between. When I met him properly for the first time, when I was around 17, I have the distinct impression that I liked him but there was not enough time in that brief interlude for me to really tell. Before I even had the opportunity to begin to find out what he was like he once more disappeared from my life and I only saw him three times after my 18th birthday.

During that short period in 1968 I guess I had asked some of the hard questions to which I had never had any satisfactory answers until then. Like, why on earth did he leave me to be brought up by the two women he presumably despised the most? He said he was an alcoholic and that at the time he believed I would be better off without him. He knew my mother and grandmother and must have known the hell he had left me in, but if indeed he had spent much of that time dependent on drink maybe he had had no choice. Of course, that did not explain why he never sent a birthday or Christmas card or present to me and why he refused to give us any financial support until I persuaded my mother to take him to court when I was 15. I told her that I would not stay on at school if she did not at least try to get some sort of support from him after all the years of struggling to provide for us both on the pittance paid to her at the cotton factory. Eventually she was awarded maintenance for me and a tiny amount for herself but he was always refusing to pay, even giving up jobs and moving around the country when the authorities tried to take the money from his salary.

What was it that made Eric Hatton think that he had no obligation to the child he had fathered and why did he have no interest in my life? As a child I distinctly remember each of his visits as yet another traumatic interlude in my troubled beginnings, but there is so little information about him to fill in the huge gaps in my understanding.

My mother tells me that she had had no interest in men as a young woman and little inclination to have any kind of relationship with my dad. Early pictures of her back in the 1940s show that she was a stunning beauty and that was probably why he pursued her in the first place. It could also have been because the family of which she was part had always had money, property and businesses! His life, according to her, had also had an unhappy start and he was probably looking for love and nurturing as much as anything else. His father was a violent man who had beaten my father mercilessly throughout his childhood. She was missing her father, who she had loved and who had died when she was 19, and was possibly looking for independent financial security, a way to escape her mother. In the 1940s most women regarded marriage as the only secure future open to them and for women like my mum who had had no access to higher education or inherited wealth it probably was. In her case it proved to be neither financially viable or, in the end, any kind of escape from her mother.

Dad was in the Royal Navy when I was born and had been all around the world on tours of duty which often lasted for months on end and he would send my mother the most wonderful notes. I found many of these recently in a box of postcards which she let me take away to look at and then gave to me. So many of these cards were from far-flung ports in other hemispheres and the loving snatches of letters which are on them seemed to reflect an enduring affection or even a deep love. The many gifts which he brought back to her, some of which I still have, belie the fact that he would later refuse to maintain her in married quarters and eventually desert her and her infant altogether. It was during one of these long tours of duty that I was born and I was eight months old when he eventually got back on dry land. He would have had to come to my grandmother's house to see us and I believe that she made him less than welcome. Whatever the reality, these visits were not happy ones.

Often children will ask parents the hard questions about the circumstances in which they find themselves living long before the adults are able or willing to elaborate. Maybe that is why I have such sketchy and vague memories of my mother's explanations of our predicament. What I do know is that she was never willing to talk about it and later it was too late – even if she had remembered. I have more and more come to realise that she was often unable or unwilling to go back to those days because of the pain she had felt.

Once I found a music box, engraved with beautiful exotic scenes of the Orient. This box came from my father and plays a haunting tune that can still reduce me to tears as I play it whilst I am typing:

'Oh, how we danced on the night we were wed...' evokes a magical, moonlit night of young love and hopeful dreams, dreams that would never be fulfilled. Mum, like me all those years later, seems to have had her dreams shattered like a fragile, frozen outline of their fairytale wedding photograph. Neither of them was able to prevent the dream turning into a nightmare.

So, Mum spoke very seldom of Dad, even when pressed for answers from a confused child who wondered where her Daddy was in an age when the only single parents most people knew about were widows. The only information she gave me about his initial absence was that she had to leave married quarters in Plymouth whilst pregnant with me because he did not give her enough money. Her only choice was to return to the North of England to live with my grandmother. Apparently in those times men in the services were asked to sign a form apportioning their pay to their wives and families and retaining the residue for their own use. This division was left to the discretion of the men themselves and presumably Daddy had kept a little too much of it – at least in Mum's eyes.

Once she, and eventually I, was ensconced in lovely Lancashire, there is little doubt that the rot had set in. She told me once, when I did finally work up the courage to ask why he never came to live with us, that it was because when he initially came back from that long tour of the Far-East I was the problem. When he picked me up, I would cry, presumably because I had no idea who he was, and that made him feel rejected. Also, he could not stand my crying in my cot either. So according to Mum it was my fault. Of course, I later came to realise that in her eyes so was everything else that had gone wrong with her life and that was so ingrained in my thinking that I came to believe it too. This was a belief that stayed with me for decades to come and helped to fuel my negative attitude about myself. Every subsequent attachment that went wrong was naturally going to be my fault; I could actually find myself to blame for most things in many circumstances. The self-hatred which stalked me for so long meant that I rejected myself very early on in life and suicidal thoughts and urges were always there until my fifties. When I was 15 I made my only feeble and, of course, unsuccessful attempt to destroy myself. The thoughts were ever with me and surfaced whenever I thought I had failed to make a success of any relationship that mattered, which was every single one, much of the time.

The healing which I have been given in greater and greater measure by the Lord over the decades has shown me that not only was I wrong to reject myself but that this too was a lie. Of course, there would be many factors involved in the breakdown of that marriage, not least my grandmother's attitude and my mother's own troubled psyche. Very little, if any, of it was to do with my infant self.

On one memorable visit – I think I was about three or four – I remember Dad trying to strangle Mum with the telephone cord after a particularly nasty row. This made his subsequent visits even more traumatic, especially as Mum still insisted that I run to this huge, intimidating, virtual stranger who appeared every few years and give him a big hug. It is little wonder that the visits dried up and stopped altogether while I was still only small. While clearing out Mum's house we found letters from him to my mother which suggested that there had been attempts on his part to be reconciled with her much later, but I never knew of these.

So, I never knew my Dad. But when I was 15 I had a nasty collision with the bumper of a car and, of course, I came off worse (the failed suicide attempt). My leg was shattered and the doctors were going to cut it off, but Mum would not let them. A strong woman, she stood up to the doctors and I am forever grateful for this. She must have had contact details for my father because he came to see me at the hospital. I get the impression that he had not believed her account of my accident, that this visit was to check its veracity more than to see if I was alright. Then when I was 17, inexplicably, he turned up again out of the blue and seemingly wanted to get to know me. He began calling for me and taking me out for meals like some hopeful suitor and we got on pretty well. These meals were lovely occasions and I really loved being spoilt and treated like an adult for the first time.

He could be extremely charming and made me feel special and I slowly began to believe that he cared about me. He made me believe that I was pretty for the first time in my life and I formed quite an attachment to him in those few short months. He eventually took me to his flat and I was able to look forward to a real relationship with him. The best thing about it was that I sort of liked him and realised we were very alike. Mum had always said I was like him but I took that as an insult because of the way he had behaved in our regard and the bitter, vitriolic way she spoke about him on the few occasions when she mentioned his name (like when I complained about home life and said I wanted to go and live with my Dad and she said he wouldn't have me).

It turned out that my love of classical music, theatre or anything cultural was from him and when he gave me an LP of piano recitals by Daniel Barenboim I was ecstatic. By this time I was in love with The Halle orchestra and would go to Manchester to see them whenever possible. Stratford-upon-Avon was my place of pilgrimage for all things Shakespearean and I dreamt of going to RADA. I sang wherever and whenever possible, performing at school, the local folk clubs and had already been in my first band. I was part of Manchester Youth Theatre and, although I never won any major parts, I loved the 'smell of the greasepaint and the roar of the crowd'. Performance was in my blood and I had, until my RTA, attended my Aunty Estelle's ballet school to become proficient in all forms of dance so that my ambition to perform in musical theatre could be realised. She had been a ballerina and once danced in the corps de ballet of the Royal Ballet.

Therefore, it was wonderful at long last to get to know this man who had fathered me. However, throughout this period of this bizarre form of 'courtship' I was on my guard and very suspicious of his motives. For reasons which will become clear in the following chapters, I never trusted men or their motives throughout my life and only in recent years have I come to see that not all men are the monsters I once suspected. This charming man, who just happened to be my biological parent, seemed to be a little too interested in me and I thought it strange that he had only become even remotely bothered as I was maturing into womanhood. Of course, this may have been simply because of my childhood experiences which I relate in the next chapter. It is certain that my opinion of and relationship with him was blighted by these experiences just as all my relationships with all men were to be for many years to come. He once told me I was not the norm for the females in his family (who were apparently very ugly). No, I was in his eyes quite attractive. Warning bells rang.

Despite my misgivings things were going so well that he came to the house sometimes and stayed to eat with us. It was after such a meal at home which Mum had cooked that this burgeoning relationship came to an abrupt and complete end.

I really don't remember what had happened or what I had said to my mother to prompt his response (probably some smart comment about the meal which was far from pleasant – by then our relationship was very strained and I was counting the days until I could leave home and escape from her). My father took a real exception to this adolescent behaviour of mine and told me not to speak to my mother in this way. What a cheek I thought. This man who had abandoned me and taken no interest in my childhood or development, who had never so much as sent me a birthday card or phoned to see if these two women he had left me with had driven me insane yet. So, I told him so. I told him that he had no right to tell me what to do or say and why, and I told him to get lost, in no uncertain terms and using language which I cannot use here.

This shocked him, shook him badly and he promptly did as I had demanded. He never came to see me again. In fact, he never contacted me and I would not have seen him again had my mother not persuaded me to have him 'give me away' when I married in 1971. Why I agreed I cannot fathom except to say that she still controlled most of my decisions, manipulating me through the guilt which I carried my whole life about her situation. I guess she wanted it so I did it.

So, Daddy disappeared again as abruptly as he had come and I learnt yet more lessons about rejection and disappointment. Blaming only myself, as usual, I stored up this failure with all the others and believed even more strongly that I was hateful and deserved nothing good in my life. This self-hatred continued for many years and was the cause of the mental health problems with which I later battled. It also made me a difficult person to get close to and meant that any happiness was ultimately doomed as I lived within the self-fulfilling prophecy that all would eventually end in tears and anyone I loved would ultimately leave me. Either that or I would betray them as Dad had done to Mum. After all, I was indeed very like him.

My Mum

There is, at last, now no doubt in my mind that Mum really did care about me. It is probable that she had always loved me although I struggled – and until very recently still did struggle – to believe this. My wonderful husband assures me that she always did, but as he grew to know her better he understood why I have always found this hard to believe. There are faint memories that when I was a tiny baby she would sing lullabies to me. Then she was as gentle and loving as possible and I remember those times like fleeting shadows in the white light glare of the childhood pain I always carried around.

She was as unpredictable as a tropical storm and often would erupt with no warning in violent and unreasonable rage or despair. She would vacillate from easy-going charm to deep depression in moments and her state of mind was unreadable and, to me as a child, incomprehensible. Only her outbursts would give any indication of where she was emotionally or mentally. I now know that she was probably suffering from mental illnesses which lay undiagnosed and untreated until her GP put her on barbiturates when I was in my teens.

When I started work in a special school, working with children who were autistic, I also realised that Mum was on the autistic spectrum and completely unable to empathise with me or anyone else for that matter. She was so egocentric that when my little scrap of humanity got in her way it is little wonder that she would knock me flying. It is also much more understandable why she was totally unable to control herself for the sake of my feelings. Added to this is the knowledge that being a single parent is very difficult and, although she only had one child and not the four which I was one day going to be left to look after alone, things were tough for her. Most of all though, I now see clearly that she was mangled emotionally and mentally just as I was by being mothered by my Nana.

So, all those years of mental torture and emotional and physical violence which happened in much the same way as David Peltzer's (and for similar reasons) were explained. In his remarkable book *A Child Called "It": One Child's Courage To Survive* he describes the same kind of treatment – albeit much more extreme – at the hands of his mother who was mentally ill and an alcoholic. I was never locked in the cellar for hours on end and starved to the point where I needed to steal food from school friends, but the same kind of rules applied. I was to be kept under control with whatever means possible and I was not to be seen to have any emotional or psychological needs. Mum did not hate me, as I believed until I was thirty. She was not evil (but I think I knew this at the time). She simply did not have the capacity to show love and to nurture a child, especially when she was struggling with her own mental ill-health.

Sadly, it did have a devastating effect on this child. Instead of home being a safe, nurturing place where a girl could retreat from the hostile world outside, it was a place of great anxiety, uncertainty and confusion. When Mum was well we could have relatively nice times, peaceful times when I could live within my fantasy world. I would be quiet and docile and be left alone to build this world, completely introvert and undemanding. At night I would long for a prince charming to climb into the window of my prison tower and carry me off on his horse Rapunzel-like.

Often, I would dream about the day the Royal Family would realise their mistake and I would be whisked off to the palace; I fantasized for years that the Queen, who was the same age as Mum and looked quite like her at around 25, was my real mother and a dreadful mistake had been made at my birth. Or Fred Astaire, who looked remarkably like my Dad, would fly me away to Hollywood where I would dance and sing all day in his wonderful films. *Daddy Longlegs* was my favourite for obvious reasons. Reality would inevitably break through though; that reality for which I longed just tantalisingly out of reach. Mum was beautiful in those days and could be really charming when in a good mood and I would sometimes be lulled into a false sense of security and find the emotional threads tightening between us. Sadly, this would not last and some circumstance of life or my childish behaviour would set her off.

Discipline was not a term used or practised in my home. There was no rule to follow, no consequence to be taken as a just result. Punishment was arbitrary and sometimes swift without any consistent reason I could ever figure out. Sometimes I was in the wrong place at the wrong time and sent flying across the room by her swift blow. Sometimes I was being 'cheeky' (which meant asking the wrong question at the wrong time, often quite innocently) and sometimes I was just looking unhappy. This particularly was not allowed as it meant I was showing my unhappiness and I would be told to 'straighten your face or I'll straighten it for you'. Most often were the verbal attacks which could be sparked for any number of offences and were truly terrifying. These went on until my fifties.

The physical violence ended much, much earlier when I was nine because of the intervention of the headmaster at my junior school. Mr Spalding saved me from further harm, at least physically, when he realised that there was something terribly wrong at home. Life with the two women who served as parents was only half of the trauma to which I was subjected, but the other half remained a secret for many years after this.

Several times during my first few years at Queen's Street Methodist junior school I would collapse on the floor, writhing around in agony and be carted off to the local infirmary. Taken by ambulance to Accident & Emergency was scary because of my fear of doctors, so this pain must have been very real for me to show any reaction at all let alone screaming in pain. Several tests and investigations revealed nothing physically wrong but the astute Mr Spalding decided to take me home and ask my mother if she could shine any light on my behaviour as these attacks were obviously acute and debilitating.

She and the good headteacher went into the front room, which was of course reserved for such visits. I have no idea why she was off work unless she had been contacted and summoned home. They talked for a while and soon after Mum and I attended several appointments at the 'Clinic' which was a sort of child guidance and assessment centre in our town. There I was taken into a room and given colouring to do and she was taken into another room to talk to someone. We never spoke of this again until I asked her many years later what they had said to her. By this time I had children of my own and understood more of the pressures which she had faced back in those days.

Now this was the late '50s and no-one told children anything so I had no idea what was going on, but after this she never hit me again. If only someone had spoken to me I could have told them about the other great assault that was taking place on me and it may have been stopped. But this was the late '50s.

Mum then had to find other ways to express her displeasure with me and, like the resourceful and intelligent woman she was, this was not difficult for her.

Perhaps the worst form of control was the emotional blackmail. This took many forms from bemoaning the awfulness of her life since she had had me (before this she seemed to have had everything she ever wanted and I had ruined that) to the threats of suicide if I really upset her. My list of crimes was long. This included complaining, being ungrateful, crying and siding with my Nana in their terrible rows, which happened daily.

These threats stayed with me for many years, buried deep in my subconscious and were only uncovered when I was ready to remember them and God was able to heal them. Why was I so terrified of deep water? Water where you cannot see the bottom? When it was safe for me to do so I remembered. When I upset her, she would threaten to throw herself in the canal if I continued. This resulted in terrifying nightmares where I would see her at the bottom of the canal with all the old bikes and supermarket trolleys. This was an effective form of control and only added to my loathing of myself and, of course, the guilt, that false sense of responsibility that her misery was my fault entirely. Like most children I loved my mother deeply and wanted to please her, not make her miserable, but this was impossible apparently.

Of course, the self-hatred was much more deeply rooted than this and the conditions for its flourishing growth in my life had begun much earlier and grown in secret for those most formative early years. My counsellor said to me once that by the age of seven we have formed the worldview and self-consciousness which will remain throughout our lives. That scaffolding onto which we then build our belief systems about life and ourselves is so crucial to the way in which we build: strong, straight, stable and secure or twisted, deformed and destructive. As the Jesuits said: ‘Give me a child until they are seven and I will give you the man’. Or in my case, give me a child until she is 10 and I will give you the woman.

In my family there was a very deep and awful secret. Not just one but several of my relatives had an unhealthy interest in very young girls. One of these was a distant second cousin who began my unusual education at a very early age when he was middle-aged, but the greatest influence was a first cousin who was not that distant to me in years but eons away from me in experience and corruption.

For most of the first decade of my life I had been given, for many hours, into the hands of my closest male relative and he used me as his plaything. This dictated to a large extent and for a very long period who I was as a person and how I grew up into a woman. Early on I had begun to see myself as unworthy of love and not a nice person, but Godfrey was largely responsible for my total self-loathing and shame, which only Jesus has been able to remove completely.

2. Hobnail Boots on Tiny Hearts

During the last few years, the media has been rocked by the huge number of allegations of sexual assault allegedly carried out by Jimmy Savile. The Yew Tree investigations have uncovered literally hundreds of cases of abuse by him and other well-known people. Now various other elderly men are paraded across our screens accused of anything from clumsy sexual advances towards grown women to the rape of a child. We live in a very different world from the 1950s and I have followed these cases with great interest and compassion for the women involved (and, incidentally, equally for the men who may have been accused maliciously and are completely innocent). More recently the footballing world has been similarly rocked by allegation after allegation of sexual abuse against young boys by coaches who were entrusted with the hopes and dreams of talented kids only to betray that trust and trample over their innocence.

Why did these victims wait so long to complain? Why were they unable to get any satisfaction from the authorities at the time if they did complain? Why were some men given access to so many vulnerable young people and able to use them as their playthings for so long with impunity? Perhaps the answer lies in the history of sexuality in this country and the attitudes towards women and girls which were, until quite recently in the UK and still in many other countries of the world, the norm.

I was born into a world where sex just was not talked about. Sex education as such was left to families and friends or was an adventure of discovery by children who were innocent, naive babes, giggling at bath times and trying to get a peek at older siblings at bedtime. Peer discussions and parents' bedroom doors left open would give clues as to what took place between couples but much of this was shrouded in mystery and mis-information. In some households there were probably wholly appropriate conversations about 'the birds and the bees' where children were guided through the minefield of sexual relationships by sensitive, articulate carers.

This was not the case in my house. Not only were there no siblings or couples, there was no acknowledgment that people had a sexual side to them. A leftover from the Victorian age into which my grandmother was born deemed that sex was 'dirty' and not to be mentioned by respectable people. Since schools were forbidden to broach this dangerous area before 11, my education was left to my older cousin Godfrey.

He took the role on with great enthusiasm and for the vast majority of my formative years coached me in the ways of the nymphet (a term I was to read of many years later in Nabokov's book *Lolita*). This had a devastating effect on all my relationships for decades, but had an overriding corrupting influence on my relationships with the male gender which has only recently been expunged from my life.

As recently as nine years ago, at the age of sixty-two, at a family reunion I was put into a situation where I had to confront this person for the first time for many years. Only by doing this was I able to see that the power he had once held over me was gone. It was possible to face him and to stand up to him and at that point I knew I was in fact free of all the results of his abuse. Healed and empowered by this new me I was able to look him in the face and refuse any physical contact. As he approached me for a hug I was even able to say, quietly and for his ears only, 'You must be joking!' and stand my ground. He did not try to touch me after that. In that short phrase I was able to say to him in fact, 'I remember what you did to me and I will never let you touch me again – you no longer have any power over me.' He understood this, and why. I am convinced that these individuals never forget what they have done, and in his case I have proof that he would have started up where he left off many years earlier.

I wonder if Godfrey has any idea of the harm he did to me. It is probably a fact that those now infamous men who had abused so many young girls (and boys) in their younger days had little regard or even awareness of the devastation they had wreaked on the young lives with which they had tampered. If they did have any real appreciation of the effect which they had had they probably justified it with the same cavalier attitude of the persistent paedophile who states emphatically (and probably with some degree of belief in the truth of what they say) that the child enjoyed the experience – therefore there was nothing wrong in their actions.

My cousin probably gave little thought to his actions at the time and may well have no idea of the trail of damage that he left. However, that does not excuse him. He may have only been a child himself when he began and an adolescent towards the end, but he knew exactly what he was doing. The terrible case of James Bulger showed us that children can behave in just as evil and as cruel a way as adults and are criminally and morally culpable. The ten-year-olds who murdered that toddler knew exactly what they were doing and were imprisoned for their crime. At ten years of age my cousin was grooming me for his future use; he was aware that in time he would enjoy the results of this.

Godfrey White was born to my mother's sister, Beryl, and Henry White, a rough and uneducated individual from the back streets of Moss Side in Manchester. Beryl had married beneath herself and, as an ex-convent schoolgirl, was living a life far from the potential which she had shown as a young girl. She was the only child in the family who had obtained a scholarship to the local prestigious grammar school at 11 and was destined for university – still unusual for women in the middle decade of the 20th century. He was definitely a non-convent boy who had charmed his way into her life and I suspect that they 'had to get married', a term used in those days for rushing into wedlock because the bride-to-be was pregnant. A 'shotgun' wedding, as it was known, was very common in the years which preceded the Swinging Sixties and the sexual revolution. A girl who 'got into trouble' married the boyfriend very quickly, if he was still around, or faced the prospect of disgrace, or of having their child brought up as their sibling or worse.

Godfrey was their only surviving offspring. My aunt had numerous stillbirths and miscarriages before and after his birth, the local Roman Catholic priest being summoned on many occasions to administer the last rites and to baptise the scrap of humanity so that its time in purgatory would be minimal. Purgatory – a strange invention of one branch of the established Church where souls languish before being consigned to Heaven or Hell, depending on the prayers (and donations!) of their loved-ones. Definitely not biblical in origin; quite the opposite in fact.

It seemed to me that their only son was allowed to roam the streets of the seaside town where they lived with his mates at all hours and that he was left much to his own devices as they worked hard and long to build up their business. They ran a busy pub in the suburbs of Blackpool. The Luton Hotel was to become a thriving and prosperous living for them and we were frequent visitors. Mum used to go over at the weekend to help them in the early years and when I was too small to help I too was left to occupy myself for most of the time when the pub was open. I had already learnt that my role was to be seen and not heard, so when I disappeared for hours at a time with Godfrey no-one questioned my welfare, if it was even thought about. It was during this time that I was found behind the bar eating the cigarettes which I had taken from the shelves; he would send me back there at a young age to filch them for him. As I grew a little older however he had an altogether different role for me to fill.

Mum told me stories of our exploits stealing cigarettes from behind the bar in the Luton Hotel when I was only around four or five. Of course, I had not started smoking at that age, hence my trying them as food, and I would sit with him as he secretly smoked our booty. It was around this time that he also started my schooling in an altogether different pastime.

As I begin the account of my relationship with this person I struggle to write about the development and ultimate results of his abuse. This part of my story is incredibly difficult to relate and in fact quite difficult to remember. Perhaps the problem with this section is that I know that, as I write, more and more memories will come flooding back – just as they have with the accounts in chapter one. Am I brave enough to embark upon this journey of remembrance? It is now more than sixty years since this all happened, but as I recall those former times it all becomes clearer and clearer in my mind. I can see the shabby wallpaper in their big back bedroom, hear the distant sound of alcohol-induced merriment seeping through the floorboards from the pub lounge downstairs and smell the beer and smoke as the fumes wafted up to the living quarters above the bars. Am I at last strong enough to go back there and relive those memories? At last, by the grace of God, I think I am.

Apparently, when I was a baby my older cousin was quite fond of me and would help to bath me and play with me. His mother and mine seemed to have got on pretty well compared to the rest of the relationships in their family which were quite dysfunctional. Even at that young age I think he was fascinated with me and saw me as his plaything. My Mum probably thought this was nice as he was the nearest thing to a sibling that I was likely to have and for many years he was like a big brother to me. She always wanted a boy (hence my name which should have been Andrew) and she doted on her dear nephew. Thankfully, not many 'big brothers' have anything approaching this kind of relationship with their 'little sister'.

Although he was only four or five years older than me, he was always the 'big boy' I looked up to, copied and admired; he alone was the one member of my family who really seemed to have any time for me or showed me any physical affection. We were children together but as I was younger and very innocent of the ways of the world he became my educator in all things pertaining to adult life. He was extremely mature both physically and socially. The latter was probably due to the life he led in the fairgrounds and penny arcades of the resort, mixing with tinkers and itinerant workers when his parents were too busy to spend time with him.

I remember we used to sit on the stairs behind the pub and he would explain to me the facts of life. He drew diagrams and sketches of the male reproductive organs for me and particularly good drawings of tiny tadpole-like creatures as they scuttled up the women's reproductive organs to make babies. Words like sperm and vagina entered my girlish vocabulary and I felt very privileged to have so much attention from this big boy. Somehow, he made it seem something private so I never mentioned these instructive talks – they were our little secret. He probably told me not to tell as he had other plans and this was just the bait. Over the next few years I even learnt to draw these pictures myself, although by some innate instinct, maybe, I never showed them to anyone. Of course, this was probably the same in many homes as older children with greater knowledge and experience told youngsters about the facts of life.

The real problem came when he decided to use a more practical demonstration of these matters and began the series of sexual assaults which took up the next three years of our relationship. It began very gently and, because I was starved of affection from anyone at home, was the only real physical contact I knew during those years that was not violent. I was so innocent and unknowing that I had no idea there was anything wrong with what he was doing to me and what he had me do to him. It became a normal, routine way of us passing the many hours when we were left to look after ourselves at night while the pub was open. The first clue that this might not be right was when Mum caught us in bed and asked what we were doing; this set up alarm bells as she seemed angry. But as she never mentioned it again I drifted back into these grooming sessions and eventually, when I was nine, Godfrey raped me.

Nobody has the ability to cope with rape. Any sexual act which is without the full, conscious and informed consent of both people is assault. The assault upon children however, even by other children or young people, is on a different level altogether. A nine-year-old does not have the mental and emotional resources to deal with sexual intercourse and I suffered in silence unable to tell anyone or even really fully understand what he had done to me.

My memory of this event is shrouded in darkness and cloud even though I am sure it was daylight when it happened. We were in my house and I think in the big double bed in the front room. At this time my mother, grandmother and I all shared one room as we had lodgers; this was the bedroom which we all shared even though it was a large terraced, three-bedroomed house. The 'lodgers' were a series of young men who were paying guests throughout my childhood as this was the only way we could make ends meet.

It is still difficult for me to remember what happened next as this memory seared a mighty scar in my mind and I have probably blocked out any other times with him. It's like a curtain has been pulled across the act, as if Providence is protecting me from seeing the awfulness of it, thankfully. Of course, there have been 'flashbacks' over the years as this trauma was undoubtedly the major trigger of the PTSD which is still being dealt with, but even these are indistinct and hazy. This was probably the point at which I began to say no to his advances and tried to avoid being alone with him. I do remember two other incidents which showed me once and for all that this could not continue and frightened me terribly.

As a young pre-teen I took to tagging on to his group of adolescent mates. These youths were typical lads and I was seen as his 'kid sister' I imagine, tolerated by them because he brought me along. Gaining some kudos from this 'relationship' Godfrey had apparently bragged to a friend of his that I liked 'messing about' and he was quite happy to pass me around. He was a pimp in the making but I was not playing. I refused his friends' advances and avoided going anywhere with him after that. Then one evening at my house an even older cousin, in his twenties, who had come to visit the family exposed himself to me as 'Godfrey tells me you like it'. This terrified me and I ran from the bedroom. He was so big and brash and I felt violated all over again. However, the fact that it was not just Godfrey who thought I would co-operate made me suspect that, somehow, I was responsible for this which added to my already well-developed sense of shame. No wonder I thought there was something wrong with me and I was indeed Nabokov's nymphet, a sexually needy child, only alive to be a man's plaything. *Lolita* is perhaps one of the evilest pieces of liberal writing to come out of our postmodern world and Nabokov has much to answer for.

There were many results of all this unwanted attention from males, not least the terrible self-loathing with which I grew up. Some of the results were particularly sad as they blighted other more positive events in my life. One particular result was the terrible fear that sex education at school unleashed.

I am not even sure that one could call it sex education. We were given a single, solitary film to watch in the first year of senior school. I was eleven and far from even the beginnings of puberty but, of course, experienced in a way no child of that age should be. This film went through some of the information which I already knew (from my cousin) but was simply all about periods and why we had them. I had passed the 11-plus exam, which at that time meant I was enrolled in the grammar school, an all-girls grammar school. Hence the emphasis on the menstrual cycle! This was really necessary because in most families, including mine, there was no advice, information or even conversation about this time in every girl's life. The necessary stuff was kept in a cupboard in the bathroom but no-one told you what it was for or why you would one day start to bleed. This was so frightening for many girls, who assumed they were very sick or dying, that the government had to begin to tell girls about their bodies and explain the menstrual cycle to them before the event occurred.

However, it was all a bit confused in my young mind and I thought that, because I had had sex at nine, when my period began I would become pregnant. I was terrified of this happening for years and I wonder if that is why my periods didn't start until I was fifteen. For the next few years the anxiety that I would be pregnant once I ovulated kept my body in a sort of hormonal limbo until the actual facts of conception were cleared up.

This was only the beginning of the terrible, long and sad journey that I was to take into womanhood. 'If only' is a phrase which I have tried to keep out of my vocabulary and thought life – there is no mileage in regrets – but sometimes I imagine what my life might have been like if this had not been my beginnings. However, and it is a big however, I doubt if I would have known the joy and peace that I have been given in these latest days on the planet and maybe I would never have been able to find my Saviour – or rather, allowed Him to find me. Despite or even because of my early life, this is a journey of discovery, excitement, amazement and elation. It is also a journey which could have been much shorter if I hadn't gone the long way round. Of course, The One who has been charting my course since long before it began knew full well that I would take a circuitous route and He has always made sure that I got there in the end. I am sure this will not cease to be the case as we continue together. First though, let me tell some of that journey and how, eventually, I got to the place where I was able to tell my story.

3. Looking for God

In the 'olden days', which I am sure is how any reader under 25 will see the 1950s, children in Great Britain were sent to Sunday school. Whilst there the morals which were then still upheld generally by most people could be imparted and a healthy fear of The Almighty and authority underscored. Parents rarely went themselves on a regular basis (unless they were middle-class and Anglican, practising Roman Catholics or actual believers in Jesus) but children were sent off each Sunday to be taught about religion and sometimes even about Christ. This gave parents a rest and the children some sort of experience of the Church (although this was not always a positive experience). In the predominantly working-class Northwest most men spent much of Sunday in the pub while their wives and older daughters prepared the massive Sunday dinner expected on their return. Sunday school helped this process along and was preferable to the small children sitting on the pub steps waiting for daddy or just getting under the feet of the beleaguered women in the kitchen back home.

My maternal grandfather was a practising Roman Catholic who had died long before I was born. My mother was not a practising anything as she had been thrown out of the Roman Catholic Church when she married my father and he refused to have me brought up a Catholic. The priest came round and unceremoniously told her never to come to church again and she never went back. This broke her heart and made her understandably bitter towards God. She had been a 'good' Catholic, going to confession each Friday before mass on Sunday – unlike her sister Beryl, who would lie about confession and go to mass anyway.

I had still been christened as a baby, probably in the local Anglican church – everyone who was considered to be 'respectable' was baptised as a baby in the '50s but that was the extent of my mother's interference in my spiritual welfare. During my primary school years I was packed off to the local Baptist Sunday school where I would learn about Jesus and sing in the choir, somehow even then realising that there was something real about this Christianity thing. Somehow, I knew that God was real. He was real in the lives of the young pastor and his wife who showed me love and care and shone with His presence. However, this was not the beginning of my 'God-awareness'.

When I was a very young child I would often pray, as many young children still do. On one occasion at that young age I had a very memorable experience of being caught up into a huge and loving embrace. As I lay perilously sick with Asian flu during the epidemic of the early 1950s it was as if I was being absorbed into something huge – bigger than the house, bigger than the world, bigger than the universe. There was a presence which was immense; it seemed to be taking me into itself with a powerful and protective embrace which tiny little me was powerless to resist. Then it let me go again as I gently settled back onto my sickbed. After this I began to improve whereas before there had been a real possibility that the influenza would take me as it had so many others. I only equated this experience with God when I had a similar experience when praying silently at a Quaker meeting many years later, after I had become a Christian.

Often when I spoke to this God (that I hoped was there) I had a sense that this was not just wishful thinking, but I had no real certainty that anyone was listening. All through my childhood I hoped that God was there but I had no proof that He even existed and certainly no idea that He would be interested in my miserable life. I was the perfect agnostic, usually ignoring a deity but hedging my bets, especially when in need!

During those years at the Baptist church I met practising Christians – the pastor and his wife were wonderfully kind and I learnt a lot about the Bible and loved the stories I heard week after week. Somehow though I could not find the answer there and at around eleven years old I decided to go to the Roman Catholic church near my house. I guess this was because my family had for the most part been part of that religion and it felt familiar to me.

For weeks I went to Sunday morning mass, loving the bells and smells and the whole theatrical flavour of it. It was more like watching a performance as the priests carried out their rituals way out at the front – disconnected and seemingly unaffected by any of us in 'the audience'. The whole thing was in Latin back in the 1960s and totally meaningless to me, so after a while I stopped going, even though I still loved the pretty pinks and pastel blues of the building. It just didn't make sense and made God seem even more remote than ever. This was a close shave as I was close to going 'under instructions' by the nuns, who would have indoctrinated me into the liturgy and beliefs of Roman Catholicism. I was to learn much later that the unbiblical teaching and practices in this particular religion make it very far from the truth of the gospel of Jesus Christ; I dread to think where I could have ended up!

At this time in my life boys became interesting to me in a much healthier way than my earlier experiences with the opposite sex. Dating began and I had my first kiss from my first boyfriend, Steve. I was fifteen and Steve was a year older. He was a good Roman Catholic boy, really sweet, and this was an innocent and childlike relationship which did wonders for my self-esteem. However, his family soon put an end to our friendship. They forbade him from seeing me – a non-Catholic – and being the sweet young man that he was he obeyed and finished with me.

This unleashed in me a terrible explosion of grief and rejection. His family had no idea that this rejection would lead me to try to end my life – of course, for I was always extremely good at hiding my true feelings, even from myself. Truly it was not just the ending of that first, sweet romance which caused me to want to die. It was just the last straw for an unhappy young girl with an abusive past battling with despair and self-hatred. I did not know it then but I had lived my life for the most part under the dark cloud of depression; that day it overwhelmed me. Only very recently have I realised that I was suffering from complex PTSD even back then and was always going to struggle with mental health issues because of a lack of understanding and diagnosis in my early life.

As I stood at the side of that busy road I gave up hope and walked out in front of the car that almost destroyed my right leg. I distinctly remember thinking as I did so (without looking to my right) that if a car hit me I did not care. I had had enough and wanted my life to stop. The explanation I gave afterwards was always that 'I was not wearing my glasses and did not see the car', but I alone knew that was a lie. At that moment I wanted to die. The poor young couple in the car that hit my reckless body were not going fast enough to kill me but the car struck my leg squarely and I bounced up in the air, landing on their windscreen and looking at their shocked faces through the glass before hitting the road.

As I lay on the ground feeling stupid and guilty and wanting to crawl away before anyone saw me, a St John's ambulanceman, who just happened to be passing, came to dress the leg which was bleeding profusely from the hole where the bones were protruding. My Godmother, Aunty Alice, who was also just coincidentally passing by, stopped to help. The ambulance siren alarmed me more than anything as I knew that people had noticed my plight; there was no creeping away unnoticed now. As I lay there beginning to feel afraid a young man with a beard and the gentlest eyes I have ever seen came and knelt at my side and took my hand. He looked into my face and held my hand until the ambulancemen took me away on the stretcher. As they gently lifted me into the ambulance I asked where he had gone but they said that there was no-one there; there had not been a young man with me at all. In the whole of the time I lay there on the road I know that He was with me and I felt no pain or fear. Just who this comforter was mystified me at the time. In the ensuing years, especially after my conversion to Christ, I have often wondered if this was an angelic visitation or Someone even more Wonderful. One day I will know, but until then I just marvel at this presence which had kept me from panic and agony as I waited for medical help.

At the hospital the surgeon who first took a look at me wanted to take the leg off. Below the knee it was fairly smashed and the bones shattered by the force of a car bumper travelling at speed. Mum would not give her permission for this and the surgeon said he would try to save the leg. She was a formidable Yorkshire woman who bravely stood up to the surgeon – unthinkable in those days! I am grateful for this as, even with all the mobility problems I have faced throughout my life, I think prosthesis in the early sixties would have been less than fun. Several hours and two operations later after the surgeon's efforts the leg was plastered up and I was taken up to the wards to recover.

During the first night in hospital I woke up with blood pouring from my face, which was quite frightening, but it was only a nosebleed and apart from that I loved my time at the local infirmary. The nurses were kind, the food was great and, best of all, I felt safe. I loved the routine, the calm and caring staff, and the ultra-clean ward with the ever-present matron who kept all things in order. Wonderful! This was probably the only time in my life, until fairly recently, that I felt a sense of well-being.

Dad turned up, bringing Mum to the hospital to see me and once more giving lie to the fact that she had no contact with him. Apparently, she always knew how to get in touch. Cynically I have since thought that he only came because he did not believe her, so needed to check that I was in fact in hospital.

After two weeks the surgeon seemed pleased with my progress and said I could return as an out-patient. Little was I to know that the leg was going to need a bone-graft in six months' time because it would not knit; that I would be in plaster for a year and that the leg would never really recover. Hardest to take at that moment though was the news that I could go home and I burst into tears when the smiling nurses told me this. I suppose they thought it was relief that caused me to sob tears of joy that I would be back in the bosom of my family. Actually, it was horror that this brief respite was about to end, that the torture of my hell house would resume very soon and I was helpless to escape.

One of the worst things about my life at home was that Nana was so two-faced and whenever we had visitors, especially when my Aunty Estelle was visiting, she was charm itself. In fact, anyone else around other than just the two of us would turn her into a gentle, loving Granny and Mum, but once I was alone with her, she reverted to type.

As I was trapped in bed downstairs unable to escape into my tiny bedroom I could not get away from Nana or my mother and there was no respite from their constant arguments – except when Aunty came. Then everyone was so nice to each other, and even to me, and one particular visit this contrast was so marked that as she was leaving I became hysterical at the prospect of the hellish behaviour continuing. Aunty Estelle, I think fearing for my sanity, took my grandmother to stay with her and not long after this dear Nana moved out altogether and Mum and I had the house to ourselves. Better still, soon I was able to go back to my beloved school and take up my quite successful academic career. Although I still needed crutches for a while the school did everything possible to assist me to return; I was actually quite popular with the staff and girls so I think they probably wanted me there. The sixth form beckoned and Mum had taken a second job to pay back my grandmother's half of the house, which meant she was working nearly all the time.

During this convalescence period Mum and I got on quite well, mostly because she was at work nearly all of the time and she was always nicer to me when I was ill. Even when I recovered she seemed to be far happier generally, probably because her evil mother was not in the house, but she was extremely tired and finally had to have major surgery and it was my time to look after her. She even bought me my first pair of contact lenses, believing as everyone else did that the car accident was as a result of my short-sightedness and aversion to glasses. It took a year for the leg to heal; a bone graft was needed after six months as there was too little bone for it to knit together, but eventually I was out of plaster, and after hard work on my part and physiotherapy it had largely healed.

It was at this point that I insisted Mum take my father to court to get some financial support as he had never contributed anything to my upbringing and it was obvious that doing two jobs was too much for her. She had always wanted me to stay on at school but I said I would only go into the sixth form if she did this, otherwise I would leave and get a job. At last we were awarded some money from the errant parent but he would constantly cease to pay. Eventually the court would put an attachment of earnings on his salary, only to see him leave his job and move on so he would not have to pay. Why he believed that he should not support his child in any way is beyond me and this is one of the reasons I never pursued any claim to an inheritance after his death. Eric Hatton never wanted me and never wanted to acknowledge me as his child. Why would he name me as his heir?

So, life was for the first time pleasant. I had a home where I felt relatively safe. I could walk again, albeit with a limp, and we had a bit more money some of the time. Then around this same time Pamela came to my school. I had passed the 11-plus and loved my time at grammar school. At last, my academic talents were recognised, giving me a big boost in self-esteem and a sense of self-worth in class at least. At school I felt secure and more or less accepted, even if most of the girls were bankers' daughters or in other ways pretty middle-class. I was quite clever and funny and many of the girls liked me. Even having to lie about where my dad was (I said he was in the Navy where he had been before I was born!) did not stop me from enjoying the sheer joy of learning and the amazing supportiveness of the teachers. These were all women, spinsters and keen to give us ambition and aspiration beyond our gender. Women who became teachers or nurses had to leave their chosen profession when they married as their role then was to look after their husbands. How times have changed!

Pam was a great girl, Liverpudlian and loud and always smelling of chips (her mum and dad ran a fish and chip shop and the family lived above the business). She and I became firm friends and we were part of a group of girls who spent all our time at school together, enjoying the camaraderie and sometimes slightly zany behaviour of this band of buddies. Funny and friendly, Pam was a popular girl with staff and pupils and I was so happy to be her friend. There was something magnetic about her and she was different from the other girls.

Her Christian faith was so integral to her life that she lived it all the time and I had not met anyone so true to their beliefs. Oh, she wasn't perfect, far from it, and she knew her failings only too well. But she was genuine and kind and above all a true believer in Jesus. Later in my life when I had left school and started down the road that was to lead me into so much pain and disappointment I often looked back on this stage in my life as my 'religious phase'. I forgot that for a season I had the first glimmerings of real faith.

Some of us would travel with Pam to the many Christian coffee bars and youth clubs which littered our region. Almost every church had a youth group and many of the cities had outreach coffee bars where young people could mix with Christians and hear the story of Salvation. This was the Swinging Sixties and despite the general liberalisation of the culture around us the massive rise of secularisation had not infected the urban landscape. The church was still central to many people's lives even if it was only to 'hatch, match and be dispatched'.

I had always been a singer. My mother tells me I first sang in public at my Godmother's wedding when I climbed up to the microphone and began to entertain the guests. I was just two. I sang at school, in assemblies I would be asked to do a solo, and in choirs made up of all the schools in the area. I sang in the local parish church as part of Christmas celebrations or at end-of-term events. I sang for school productions and concerts and had already been in my first band by the time I was fifteen, loving the attention and applause we would generate in wine bars and workingmen's clubs. At every opportunity and whenever asked I would sing. It was what made my life worthwhile and worth living. It was how I survived. This was God's gift to me to help me keep going throughout my traumatic childhood, although I didn't know it at the time. It also became a way of defining who I was as a person, as something other than a sex object.

When Pam and her friends asked me to sing with them at various Christian events it only seemed natural to say yes, even though I knew that when they gathered together to pray before or afterwards, somehow, I was missing something.

Some of the time I felt part of the group but mostly I was an outsider who somehow did not understand what was going on. After my feeble attempt at self-destruction, I had settled into this new kind of life and enjoyed the friendship and sense of belonging. The Holy Spirit was at work in my heart and He began to draw me to Himself through this until one memorable day he spoke to me very clearly. Christians were different from other people, this was obvious, but I had no idea that God was in fact the reason why. He was real, living in His people and Lord of the whole world. He was about to invite me to become part of His story in such a dramatic way that I could not deny His reality. Sadly, however, I was able to deny Him.

I was seventeen and dressed only in black and white. This attire was very like the more modern 'Goth' look, although instead of the jet-black look of the Goth I only used henna to colour my hair a sort of rusty red. I remember that I was wearing a long, black, leather coat which was my usual outfit outside school. I still remember where I was, walking home from my voluntary work at the hospital at the top of 'The Avenue'. This end of the road where I lived opened out into a wide road with a medium-sized traffic island and I had just crossed over towards my house when God spoke to me. Oh, no heavenly voices rumbled from above. In fact, there was nothing audible at all, but He spoke. Deep within me there was a soft and strong insistent voice of authority and I knew who it was. I had after all been looking for Him all my life.

'Give me your life, now', the voice said and I was so sure of the reality I replied out loud. I answered Him as clearly as He had spoken to me. Stupidly though I answered no. 'No,' I said. 'Not yet. I want to go and live my own life first.'

I have often heard it said that God is a gentleman so therefore He will never force Himself onto anyone. Perhaps it is rather that He wants our willing acceptance of the invitation He makes for us to live in friendship and peace with Him. Without this willingness He is unable to do the necessary work of cleaning up those broken lives with which we come to Him. So, of course, He will not force the relationship onto us.

He therefore allowed me to do exactly what I had asked from Him. For the next ten years I walked further and further away from the Lord, His ways and His will and He allowed me to do just that.

During this decade I became an adult with all the so-called freedom and subsequent dangers which came with that in the Swinging Sixties. I made such a mess of my life, basing my decisions on the warped and twisted view of myself and the universe which was the result of the awful childhood I had had and my own flawed, selfish human nature. Sometimes my children remind me of some of these decisions as they are living now with the results of some of my mistakes, which we still face in the present. My decisions did not only affect my life but also those whom I loved. This sadly is one way in which the 'sins of the father are visited upon the children'!

Needless to say, after I said no to the Lord, I lost my closeness to Pam. In fact, things began to change rapidly after this fateful decision. Instead of looking for a loving Heavenly Father who would look after me, heal the hurts from my past, and give my life true meaning and purpose I began to look for a man who would fill all these roles. Obviously, this person does not exist and, like so many women before me, I was to find that out only too quickly.

My life began to spiral out of control and I found a new set of friends who were not as caring and safe as the Christian group I had spent so much time with. Boyfriends became my preoccupation although singing was always very important and I would travel around the country, sometimes hitch-hiking, singing at various folk clubs and looking for meaning in the music and counter culture of the day. Hitchhiking was a common form of travel for the young in the sixties although I was never stupid enough to go alone. Even so, I am sure I would not always have been safe if Someone was not still keeping a protective eye on me.

There were some very dubious people in the circles in which I now moved but I did not care. Reckless and blind I was stumbling along towards destruction as when I walked out in front of the car – only this time it would take longer to hurt myself and the damage would be more invisible. Much later, when going through some training for counselling, I learnt that survivors of sexual abuse often take unwise risks in their later life. Tragically some of these decisions meant that I would not only hurt myself through particularly bad decisions but those around me and generations still to come. I had stopped looking for a creator, my kind and wonderful Heavenly Father who I had always dreamed about. He had given me the freedom to go and live my own life just as I had asked him to do but He did not abandon me. He still had plans for my life but these would have to wait until my circumstances and my many mistakes had brought me to a place where I would finally say yes to Him.

4. Two Weddings and a Funeral

When you are seventeen with a large amount of emotional baggage, an abusive childhood and looking for love it is highly likely that it is not love that you will find. Predatory humans are everywhere and they are always looking for vulnerable young men and women to take under their wing. Problematically I did not know I was vulnerable; I just thought I was a mess and hoped no-one would notice behind my mask.

Men were plentiful, so many of my female friends dated men much older than themselves in the constant search for an exciting life of fast cars, expensive restaurants and trips away, with the necessary payment required. This payment took various forms but rarely resulted in the 'lived happily ever after' of Walt Disney's fairytale princesses. In fact, I doubt that they or their 'Prince Charmings' were very interested in happy-ever-after scenarios. These creatures were true children of the Swinging Sixties and the sexual revolution, but I was not interested; I was looking for love but had absolutely no idea what that was supposed to look like. It was great to have a boyfriend to take me out but I was unwilling to become involved in any kind of serious activity with the opposite sex, so I would always back off when the date became too heated or physical. After my traumatic experiences with Godfrey and the other deviant members of my family I was scared of physical intimacy and this kept me safe from exploitation. This failsafe reaction was necessary as I only saw myself as an object of male pleasure; this would have made me open to exploitation if I had not been so afraid of men. This created a terrible internal conflict which did little for my emotional wellbeing and nothing at all for my suitors. Oh, there were young men that were decent and quite nice and ready to treat me with respect and care but none of them suited me as well as the result of my first and last blind date when I was eighteen.

I was working near my home town as an auxiliary nurse at Warwick hospital, housed in an old lunatic asylum from the Victorian age. It had been re-opened as a home for children and adults with mental disabilities in the 1950s having originally been an institution for the holding and repairing of the mentally ill. The building reflected the shadows of that unpleasant fact. The corridors were grim affairs more reminiscent of Colditz than a hospital and the grey forbidding buildings were austere and gloomy. However, this was my first real work with children and, horrible setting apart, I loved it.

The job started while I was in the sixth form; it continued throughout my years at teacher training college and, along with savings Mum had started for me in my childhood, allowed me to save up the funds for a deposit on my first house. This job was part-time which meant that I paid no tax, so my monthly pay packet was more than my monthly salary in my first year of teaching. I loved the children on the children's ward but was shocked to see the conditions which prevailed in the adult section. Men and women were segregated except during the church service on Sunday morning; all the inmates spent much of their time doing nothing. Even the children had little stimulus or interaction with adults that did not consist of meeting their daily needs for feeding, washing and changing. Happily during my time there the on-site school opened and joyous boys and girls marched out of the house unit into the school house eager to learn, to meet with their friends and teachers – to go to school. It was there I first saw the result of mental disability and it shocked me. What shocked me more was that many of the children had milder learning difficulties but had been abandoned by their families and left to vegetate there. The work was heavy and testing but a great improvement on the hand car wash that had been my first job at fifteen!

It was outside this workplace that I was to meet my first and only blind date; blind dates were then a common way for people to meet up as the age of online dating had not yet dawned. Sometimes people did put adverts in the paper but the people you were then likely to meet were always likely to be a bit dodgy. Mostly you went out with your friend's brother, a boy from the local disco or someone you went to school with; this was difficult for those of us at all-girls' schools!

I cannot remember who our mutual friend was but I still remember being picked up for the first time in his father's Daimler when the date after work had been arranged. Clive was good looking in a conventional way, with a quiet mature demeanour. The strong silent type, I guess, who genuinely seemed to like me, who could understand where I was coming from. I fell head-over-heels from the start. He was at a Yorkshire university studying materials technology – a scientist and quite different from the arty drama types I was used to. He obviously fell for me too – although his family weren't so sure – and we 'courted' throughout the summer break. Courting was a strange, archaic term looking back; oh, so very different from the way relationships are worked out today. You would go to the pictures (cinema), maybe for a drink (orange juice or sometimes an adventurous Babycham) and always walk the girl home (because you were not likely to have a car and we could not afford taxis). After a while both sets of parents would be introduced to the girlfriend/boyfriend but would never actually meet one another until the engagement was official.

When we both returned to Yorkshire at the beginning of term, we found that the college where I was training and his uni were a mere half-hour drive apart and we became inseparable, spending most weekends together at one or other of the two. He had an old banger to drive over in and sometimes I would get the bus for the hour-long journey to his city just so that we could be together. It was not long before Clive proposed and we planned to marry when I finished college, which would probably have worked out quite well if I had not changed his mind and consequently our wedding date. My best friend was getting married in the summer break before our final year and so I persuaded Clive to bring our date forward a year to coincide with hers.

There was just one slight problem in all of our revised plans – the corner shop that his mother ran in the tiny town where he had been born and brought up.

He was a year ahead of me at university but had promised his mum he would go home for a year after he graduated to work for his keep in her shop.

This was a pretty unimpressive corner shop at the front of their house, just the original front room really. They sold groceries, basic foodstuff with a few extras like cigarettes. I didn't see why he would need to work there at all as it was hardly a thriving business so I persuaded him to bring the wedding forward a year as I did not want to spend that time alone in Wakefield finishing my studies. I told him the reason was that my best friend was getting married that year so of course I wanted to do the same; I probably could not admit to myself or him the fact that I could not be alone, would not cope with living alone and was so dependent on him. He took little persuading; his parents were told and as they seemed to accept the fact that he would not be coming home for a year we went ahead with the planning for our nuptials.

Looking back this was a very silly way of organising my life but that was me – immature and emotionally crippled and, at the age of twenty, unable to think of existing on my own in a small flat in the nearest city; crucially, in every way imaginable, I was extremely selfish. Clive had become my security blanket, he would comfort me when I would often cry inconsolably, overwhelmed as I often was by the fears and depression which dogged me. He was the first and, up until then, only person that I had told about Godfrey. He seemed to really care about the terrible affect which this wrought on me and was still negatively impacting my life. This dependency left me unable to think of existing without him and I only saw the way things would affect me, having little or no concern for the way this might impact Clive and his family. This decision was to cost me dearly and ruin whatever chance of happiness we might possibly have had.

We were very young – I was 20 and he was 21 – but we thought we knew everything, as young people often do. In our own little world we were pretty happy most of the time. We seemed to have the same mind on everything and there was little conflict in our relationship. Hindsight is a wonderful thing is it not? It is obvious to me now that Clive was too weak to stand up to me, giving in with little or no resistance so that I always had my own way. Of course, he was probably scared of upsetting me. I was emotionally mangled and prone to bouts of deep melancholy and needed him to provide my security and support. In the biggest of decisions, the one that was to affect our future lives together, he would appear to give me my own way. But behind the scenes things were very different.

The wedding went well despite my having to make my own dress, which actually turned out to look pretty professional. In spite of my misgivings, I gave into my mother's request that I have my dad give me away. This was bizarre really as he had thrown me away at birth, but to please her I said yes. She had worked hard to keep me at school and, as with every other aspect of my life, was paying for the wedding herself, so I really could not say no.

The honeymoon was amazing, travelling through Europe by train until we got to Zurich where we stayed for a while. My dad even took us to the station, gave us a large gift of money (which was probably why my mother wanted me to ask him to give me away) and we set off for a wonderful time. At last, here was someone I could rely on who would always be there, would always look after me and keep me safe. Here was a man who was going to stay with me, forever caring for me. Clive was the epitome of a dependable and reliable husband and would never leave me or let me down. Or so I thought.

It turned out that the future life we had planned, for which I had longed, that the days that lay ahead were not going to pan out exactly as I had dreamt. They were going to be very different.

During the weeks before the August wedding Clive and I had been busily preparing for our life together as newly-weds. We had sought and found a lovely little first-floor flat in a wonderful Georgian square in the nearest city to my college. We signed the letting agreement – or actually, he probably did as he was the man and women still had little chance of being recognised as the formal tenant in any agreement where a husband was to be involved. Many of the other apartments in the square had been rented by students, some of them from my college, a few were even good friends. The setting was idyllic as the Georgian square where we were to live was just far enough away from the bustling centre of the city. It was surrounded by gardens, in the centre of which was an old church building which had a charming Gothic beauty.

This city was a short bus journey from my college. Clive's old banger had died a death but when he got a job we would buy another so that he could pick me up from late rehearsals and performances. He had his degree; I would soon be a qualified teacher; the world would be our oyster. Although it was only a large bed-sit really with a shared bathroom and kitchen along the corridor, the flat was very suitable for students and only £2 a week. In 1971 this was equivalent to about £30 a week today but this was still very cheap. These were the days when young couples had to make do with furniture from relatives and we had happily furnished it from bits and pieces donated by family or discovered in second-hand shops and the prize piece of furniture was a huge double bed which dominated the room. The enormous bright orange candlewick bedspread that had been mine made the room look cosy and bright. The fact that nothing was new or particularly stylish never bothered us one bit. We were going to be together and that is all that mattered.

There was a real, coal fire in the main bedroom; this also doubled up as a sitting room and I looked forward to cosy nights together sitting by this in the coming winter. Heaven! So, in mid-September we were due to move in and really begin our married life in our first home. Financially things would be a bit tight until he got a job but I had been receiving a full maintenance grant throughout my training and we were in love. Money was irrelevant!

What actually happened was completely different to my idealised picture of our first year together. It began the day we returned from our wonderful first holiday, the day the honeymoon ended in more ways than one. We had been married for just two weeks.

It must have been the evening of the day we arrived back in Clive's home town after this amazing trip through Northern Europe. We had taken the train as far as possible on our budget, loving the journey and relishing the sights and cuisines of all the countries through which we had passed. We had grown closer than ever and I had become totally dependent on him and this relationship.

I think there were a few days left of my summer break, which we were going to spend at his house before returning to Yorkshire. The timings are all hazy but I don't think we had been back long, possibly only a day or so. When Clive's dad picked us up from the station he seemed a little distant. I thought this was strange as we had always been quite close; it was his mother I had always struggled to get to know, but I always put this down to the fact that we had nothing in common except her son.

I vividly remember that I was sitting by the fire in Clive's parents' lounge. I can even picture the scene all these years later so seared onto my memory is the unfolding of the next few hours. The living room was a small affair at the back of the house with a tiny kitchen tacked onto it. The 'front room' had been converted into a small grocery shop years before where his mother had worked for many years while his dad was out at his job of electrical repairman. It was her domain; neither Clive nor his younger sister worked in it as their schooling was seen to take precedence over serving in the business. Looking back, this shop was probably the financial difference needed to keep both children on at school thus giving them the opportunity to go on to higher education, something none of our parents could even have dreamt of.

This was the shop, small and tatty in my eyes, that Clive had once promised to work in for a year when he had finished university. I had often helped him on Saturday mornings delivering groceries to local families long before online shopping had become the vogue. Clive and I had talked about the promise which he had made to his mum; we also talked through the fact that his parents had released him from it when we had decided to marry that year. When we had first broached the subject with them their first thought was that I must be pregnant, but we put them straight at once! The fact that this was now all arranged was absolutely clear in my mind; we had put our wedding plans forward, agreeing that we should both move back to Yorkshire and live together as man and wife, but this apparently was not the case. It never had been.

On that first evening back from our wonderful holiday Clive's mother had gone to bed – in a cowardly fashion as it turned out – and it was left to his father to break the news. As the three of us sat around the fireplace, relaxed and comfortable after our evening meal, his dad made the amazing statement. My husband was not coming with me the following week when I returned to Yorkshire to begin my final year. He was staying to work in the shop for his mother for the year, as promised, and I would have to go alone. Clive would drive me over there in his dad's car, with all my suitcases, but then he would return to his parents for the rest of my time in college.

I remember little of what happened next except that I became hysterical, screaming and sobbing and promising that she would never hold my children on her knee. I cursed the woman who had ruined my marriage and any hope of happiness. I was inconsolable. Not daring to upset me by keeping to our original plans but unable to let his mother down by breaking his promise to run her business for a year, Clive had allowed them all to deceive me into thinking that all would be well. His lack of backbone was apparent so clearly at that time, or was it that I was such an emotional cripple that he could not risk saying no?

When I finally awoke exhausted from a fitful night's sleep the darkness of depression once more overwhelmed me and I could barely function. Yet again the man in my life was going to desert me, even though I had partly brought this upon myself; in my mind it was as if he was leaving me. I could not deal with it.

Clive had obviously been unable to tell me that we could not marry; to his credit he was not prepared to let his family down by pulling out of his commitment to the shop so this was the family's solution. I actually do not think he was given much of a choice in the matter. The shop had to be looked after and she could no longer manage this for reasons which became obvious later; the woman was ill and was diagnosed with cancer only a few years afterwards. The work in the shop was long and heavy, had become too much for her to cope with but she was unwilling to close it down as it had been her life for so many years.

However, I knew nothing of this, only seeing the affect that this was going to have on me. If I had known, I doubt it would have made much difference as I was extremely selfish, self-centred in the extreme and only seeing how this was going to affect me. I never even wondered what Clive was going through just wildly wondering how I could cope alone. Deception and betrayal were all I could see and once more a man who I should have been able to rely on had let me down.

Cold, dark tentacles like the curling poison of a small, black jellyfish wrapped themselves around my heart as the misery of yet more rejection settled on my soul. Although I did not realise it until years later, from that day on I was looking for someone else. As far as I was concerned Clive and I were finished. Something in me died. Hope again was crushed and I was going to be abandoned. As always I was far from in touch with my feelings and at the time knew only that the situation was making me ill. Ironically only a few months earlier I had tired of my studies and toyed with the idea of not finishing the course. It was only the sacrifices my mother had made to keep me there that spurred me on to the final year.

Less than a week later Clive returned me to the flat, drove back to his parents' town across the Pennines, and left me to numbly go through the motions of living. This was going to be for a year but I struggled with coping for the first few days. My memories of that time are very hazy. I simply remember sleeping lots, crying when I was awake and doing little to pursue my studies. In fact, the overwhelming memory is of my lying in that big bed for hours on end with the orange bedspread grasped in my hands while life passed me by. Clive came over at weekends to visit me and we pretended that all was well but really our marriage was over on my side even if I did not recognise it. As ever, the disconnect between me and what I felt allowed the idea to form that we could continue to be together even though now he was more like a brother to me or a friend.

In fact, the whole arrangement with his parents fell apart very quickly when Clive and his family realised that he was going to have to support me financially anyway because the powers-that-be had cut my grant to a tenth of its value that year. A married woman's grant was a mere £275 a year as her husband was expected to support her as a student and she became dependent on him financially as soon as they were married. Even in the early 1970s this was not going to be enough.

I had no money. Clive had no paid work as he was working for his mother for free for the year and my mother could not afford to keep me which was why I had received a full maintenance grant for two years. Here I was, stuck in Yorkshire, with no husband, no money and no way to finish college. The only way out was to leave college and live with Clive at his family home which would not work now that my relationship with his mother had broken down completely. So, he came back to me. Expedience was the real motive for this return, not care or concern for my welfare. That did little for our relationship. We were living together, after only a few weeks, but we were never really together again. My heart had been broken; it was not going to mend just because he had decided to come and live with me. Whether it was his decision or once more his parents who had told him that he must come I do not know, but he came. There was no reconciliation, no making up, in fact no talking about the incident at all. We never dared to even broach the subject, rather pretending that the incident had never happened. We 'brushed it under the carpet' with any other issues we may have had until it became a very lumpy road on which we were trying to walk together.

The first few years were not too bad but, as I said earlier, we were living more or less as friends – all hope of intimacy was gone and never returned. I finished my course and got a job in a large comprehensive school, while he got a good job in his field and we were financially set up. We bought a shiny new sports car, a small house and went on wonderful holidays abroad, but I was miserable. Affluent and fancy free, we should have been happy but both of us knew really that our relationship was irreparable. Teaching was stressful, the marriage a sham and so, very gradually, drinking became my only pleasure.

I had always drunk to numb reality, finding that nice fuzzy feeling a great deal more pleasant than being sober, but now I would drink most evenings until reality faded. Only then would I be released from all the tensions and fears that beset me. Somehow I escaped complete addiction but I was definitely dependent on alcohol and it affected my behaviour and decisions badly at times. Singing, which had been my saviour all my life up until now, had gone out of the window and I had not been in a band or in fact done any performance since I got married. Once I left college all hopes of a career in the performing arts was dead and depression once more overwhelmed me. Alcohol became a very good friend because through its influence I was able to limp through life from drink to drink, enjoying more and more the sense of freedom that being inebriated brought. I missed the singing but knew from bitter experience that the 'happy hour' performance was not my best and it was far better to keep silent than humiliate myself off key and slurry.

Then Clive told me about a friend at work who was in a band and we went to see them play. Surprisingly they were quite good but lacked a real lead singer. When he suggested I sang for them I did not take much persuasion because at heart I was still a performer. They loved my voice and with encouragement from my husband I was soon their newest member and lead singer.

John was the only member of the band to whom I could really relate. He was a bit younger than me and had not long started work after walking out of his A-levels once he had written his name. His parents had pressured him to do sensible science subjects, which he hated, for A-level; that explained his inability or unwillingness to stay for the actual exams. A bit of a rebel, he appealed to my rebellious nature and I found him easy to talk to and so very different from Clive. He was artistic and sensitive and I was soon smitten.

We were great friends at once but I wanted more and decided to win him. I have found to my great sorrow that this never works. In my own life and in the life of many others I have seen that people need to be mutually drawn to each other and that it rarely works out well if one person pursues another. After a few short months I was sure that I could not stay married to Clive and I wanted John to move in. The fact that I was already married meant nothing to me; the relationship had been platonic for the most part since I had felt deserted by him straight after the honeymoon. We really were more like brother and sister. There was, in my mind, no external reason to stay married and many of the marriages in my little world were short-lived. As in the rest of Western culture, my experience of and attitude to the institution was very different from its ideal.

To his credit my husband was sympathetic when I told him all of this. We were, after all, still good friends and Clive actually went to get John one evening so we could all talk the situation through. He even suggested we could all live together. A 'ménage à trois' was a new phenomenon in English society and I am not sure he was serious, but it was not going to happen however bohemian our lifestyles were. As soon as Clive realised this, he said he would move out because he wanted me to be happy; he had a real concern for me and he knew I had been miserable for a very long time. Of course, it may also have been because he lacked the strength to put up a fight for us, if in fact there was an 'us' left at all; I suspect that he could not face the stress of this, or even just the continuing trauma of living with a neurotic me.

John moved in soon after and we became a couple. Mum's reaction was fairly typical. When told about this new arrangement she simply wanted to know what would happen to her if my new partner didn't like her – who would look after her? No surprise there then. The self-centred mother I knew would never be able to see my life spinning out of control, just its effect on her. I understood this completely; after all, I was exactly the same.

Despite my inability to connect with my emotions and a complete lack of any kind of belief system, I knew that what I had embarked upon was wrong and doomed to failure, fearing that John would leave me eventually. I remember telling Clive that one day I would be looking for someone like him; someone who truly cared for me the way a husband should. Really, I knew that this was going to be one of the worst decisions of my life, in keeping with my self-destructive nature, but could do nothing to escape once I had set my stupid heart on the relationship.

John and I both gave up our jobs and embarked upon a fairly chaotic, hedonistic existence with the band taking more and more of our time. There were camping holidays on the beach and endless nights out. We performed all over the area in wine bars and clubs but the other band members were so appalled at our new living arrangements they kicked us out, which broke the band up. Once more my bad decisions and corrupt lifestyle ruined my chances of a successful singing career. We both got shop work and dreamed of becoming self-sufficient, of living on a smallholding in the Shetlands. We would undoubtedly have starved or frozen to death long before we learnt how to survive. What a pair of self-centred, lazy, irresponsible dreamers we were.

In this haze of lack of accountability and responsibilities we were very happy in our dead-end jobs for a while. We had a great social life, partying with a new set of friends who shared our simple ethos of live for today and look after number one. When I look back now I wonder how we could have been so fancy free. I was living in a wrong relationship and I knew it but I suppose I buried that deeply inside with all the other rubbish and refused to deal with it. Sadly, I did not much care what anyone else in my life thought or how this had affected them. I was ok and that was all I cared about. Complacent and content in my stupidity for the most part there was always this nagging feeling that this could not last but I pushed it away and careered ahead. Living for the moment and not concerned about the way our lives impacted on others, John and I sang in many folk clubs with our friend Terry and we even had a few paid bookings. John seemed happy too and our life was fairly uneventful. We even joined Friends of the Earth and became environmental activists in a small way, vegetarian and 'New Age' in so many of our attitudes. We got on so well – both selfish and full of our own self-importance – we agreed on so many issues which took our interest.

My friends from college were more tolerant of my lifestyle than the band had been. Life at a drama college had made us all immune to the social mores of our day which themselves had corrupted significantly since the Swinging Sixties and we believed this was the dawn of a new era of personal morality where one was not answerable to any other set of values than one's own. The old lie of 'as long as you don't hurt anyone else anything goes' was our get-out. Like many other humanists I thought that if I kept to my own moral code I was truly moral myself. Of course, I really did not keep to it at all well and it was highly suspect anyway!

The insidious growth of humanist philosophy was probably at its strongest in our academic institutions and students were at the forefront of the change of values and the behaviour that came with it.

So old colleagues from teacher training college regularly invited us round to see how well they were doing, especially one friend, Liz, and husband Pete who had produced adorable twin boys. John did not really know them so my best friend Pauline came with me and an amazing thing happened.

Pauline and I, friends since we began college, were both fairly independent, career-minded women who, before the visit, were both modern twentysomethings who thought that we would never, ever, want children. We were the new breed of late twentieth century women who had little time for small children and even less time for staying at home to look after them. Women who did become mothers in the mid-seventies still usually stayed at home to look after them, consequently their careers took a nosedive. Maternity leave was only a shadow on the horizon and maternity pay a joke; nurseries were where seedlings grew into plants.

Pauline and I had both tasted the freedom that financial independence brings to women when they have a career. Even though I was not teaching by this time I was in retail management and I loved my little shop. There was no way that I would want to be dependent on a man; in my experience they could not be depended upon in any context. This visit to our mutual friend was to change everything forever for us and afterwards, inexplicably, we both went to our respective homes completely and utterly 'smittled' – this Yorkshire term defined as a totally, all-consuming and irresistible need to have a baby. Apparently, this is a common phenomenon when childless women of child-bearing age meet gurgling, chubby, contented babies.

The inevitability of the biological onslaught when I returned from that visit shocked me. I had to have a child. I wanted to be pregnant. Baby, baby, baby was all I could think about. The obsession was total. At 26 my body was on the clock and knew it and there was nothing I could do to reverse the process. When I told John, far from running a mile, he was all for it so I came off the pill and almost immediately became pregnant. We were ecstatic; our little foray into self-sufficiency was all but over and he got a proper job in order to support us both and we prepared, as all young couples do, for the arrival of our baby. A kind of normality returned to our lives and we gave up the idiotic plans to own our own smallholding – just as well as undoubtedly this would have led to our complete ruin or worse had we pursued our disastrous dreams.

Although I did not know it at the time Someone else was also preparing for the arrival of our son. Throughout the previous nine years I may have turned my back on God but He had not forgotten me and the circumstances were all being put into place to give me that second chance to say yes to Him. His plans and purposes are fantastic as He directs the course of our lives when we are not even aware of His existence.

John had been working at a jeweller's shop at some point during the four years before our baby boy was born. Through this work he had met a young businessman called Chris who was a working jeweller with his own retail outlet. Chris was married with two young children and during the pregnancy our two families became firm friends. They invited us to parties at their wonderful home. This was an enormous dwelling, a converted barn which made our tiny terraced house look like a hovel. As a working jeweller Chris was fairly affluent; his wife came from money so they had everything a young couple could want. Although we envied their lifestyle, we thought they were a little odd as they professed to be Christians and spoke about 'the Lord' as if he was a real person who lived with them. Even odder was when they left our thriving metropolis and moved to an inner-city area of a large Yorkshire city. They were friendly people who would pop round to see us despite living a half-hour car journey away and they soon became really good friends. Felicity, Chris's wife, was especially kind when she realised how scared I was about the birth and gave me a card on which she had written a verse from the Bible that she hoped would give me some comfort:

"Have I not commanded you? Be strong and courageous. Do not be terrified; do not be discouraged, for the LORD your God is with you wherever you go." Joshua 1 v 9

Although I laughed about it when she had left, I put the card in my case which was packed ready to take into hospital when labour started. At the time the significance of this promise was lost on me but when I believed in my Saviour this verse in Joshua became – and all these years later is still – part of the bedrock of my life.

The day came and we went off to the delivery ward. Terror seized me so completely that it took 24 hours for the birth. I was still hoping for a natural childbirth without pain relief but eventually the doctor insisted on an injection to help me to relax – pethidine, which produces an amazing high where the pain is there but you just do not care.

At last, with a light flurry of snow dusting the morning scenery, Isaac John was born on April 12th 1978. This single event convinced me that all other experiences before it had been totally inconsequential. It was without a doubt the most important thing that had ever happened to me. John and I were both bowled over by this tiny screaming scrap of humanity and the unparalleled experience of becoming parents. Remember he was only in his early twenties and I, although a few years older, was emotionally retarded.

I did not know what had hit me. For all the months of longing for a baby I had not had the slightest idea how the reality was going to overwhelm me and after a few days I realised this was not going to be a situation that I could deal with. For one thing he did not stop crying, especially when I held him. He wanted feeding all the time and would not settle. Once we came home and I was left alone with him for hours on end I feared I would not cope. Not only did the new father go to work to feed the family, John still went out at night with our friends, leaving me alone with this crying baby for most of the time. He was not coping any better than me but he could escape the nest and this he did whenever possible.

Like a slowly building tsunami, a rising panic threatened to overwhelm me. This panic overpowered any feelings of love I may have had, making it harder and harder to bond with my baby boy. When his dad picked him up Isaac would calm down, go to sleep eventually, even seem happy, but when I was alone with him there was no rest. We were both inexperienced, neither of us had ever held a new-born before let alone cared for one. We did however know a couple who seemed to be able to do this parenting thing really well.

Chris and Felicity's two little girls were adorable and these new friends seemed to enjoy being parents. We realised that we did not and so we would drive over to see them several times a week. By this time they had left the wonderful barn conversion and gone to live on a big city, high-rise housing estate. Chris was acting as caretaker for the church hall on the estate which meant they were living in the accommodation which came with the job. Their little flat was a far cry from the opulence they had left and we were intrigued. Rumour had it that when they sold up they had given most of the money away so that now they were living in relative poverty. What would make a rich young man give up his home and business to train for the Anglican priesthood?

So, we went week after week until the day when Isaac was six weeks old. At their home we found a kind of peace and stability that helped us to cope with baby trauma. In fact, the baby did seem so much easier to deal with when we were there. We tried to confine our conversation to baby-related things but eventually curiosity about their new lifestyle overcame our unwillingness to get too involved in their strange beliefs. That night, after the children had gone to bed and Isaac had finally gone down for a sleep, we asked what had made them embark on such a dramatic change. As if he had just been waiting for this request Chris told us his story, how at thirteen he had become a Christian and been born again. How at a meeting in his twenties he had been filled with the Holy Spirit and spoken in tongues and decided he should become a vicar. I nearly laughed out loud at this last bit; they really were fruitcakes and he the fruitiest. But instead, I bit my tongue and simply said that if I was going to believe in God then He would have to give me a miracle. Little did I realise that in order for that to happen I was literally going to have to say goodbye to all my pre-conceived ideas and commit my old life to a funeral pyre!

5. Beginning Again

Today's world is a very different world from the time when I was born. Aggressive secularisation has been described as rampant in our land and throughout the developed Western world. This is undoubtedly true. Only 50 years ago almost everyone in England had a respect for God. Even if they did not believe in any kind of deity most people thought religious observances were important. Very often that just covered hatching, matching and dispatching. Babies were always christened; people generally got married, in church, before living together and always before having children. Respectability and the established Church went hand in hand and when being buried a Christian service was most people's insurance policy where the possibility of an afterlife was concerned.

In 1978 when I threw out my challenge to the Almighty to prove His existence to me things had already started to slide in British society so I was well on the slippery path of atheistic cynicism which now pervades every area of life in 21st century Europe. God was a joke to me and I was mocking Him and His deluded followers with my reaction to this silly person's beliefs. As far as I was concerned he and his wife were a little mad. Happy, but totally dotty. Amusing in their daft lifestyle that seemed an even bigger joke to me. God however was seemingly not amused.

John and I had been waiting for Isaac to wake up for a feed before we went home. This he normally did with unrelenting regularity every two hours but just for once it was over four hours and Chris's long, drawn-out account had filled the gap admirably. I had just given my arrogant response that God would have to prove His existence to me when Isaac awoke, demanded milk and was catered for. We hurriedly changed him, setting off for home at a little after midnight.

The night was still and clear. It was Whit weekend, Pentecost in the church calendar, and Isaac was just six weeks old. He lay fast asleep in his carrycot which was strapped in the back seat (this was before the days of child car seats). Late May in North Yorkshire is usually pleasant and there was no cloud over the winding A-road north. I was in the passenger seat as always and we were going to be home in around half an hour.

Slowly I became aware of a strange tingling sensation, a bit like a benign electric current which began at the top of my head and ran through my whole body. It was not unpleasant, just strange and unlike anything I had ever experienced in my 27 years. I whispered to John what I was experiencing and he said he had the same sensation. I realised something odd was happening to him as he had slowed the car right down, gripping the steering wheel as if his life depended on it. His usual relaxed easy-going style of driving had come to an abrupt end and he looked extremely tense. Almost straight after this I realised I was actually scared – not just nervous or worried about the situation but truly frightened and I looked into the night sky to see a shimmering glow all around us, reaching from one end of the horizon to the other like a giant, translucent, colourless rainbow.

This was the Presence of God and I knew it … and I was afraid. I knew that this Being was completely Holy. Perfect. Spotless. I on the other hand was made aware how completely corrupt my life was in comparison – almost able to see the blackness which covered both of us. This utterly terrified me.

By this time we were halfway home and entering a slightly more built-up area. The light faded and the 'Presence' seemed to fade a little but as we got out into the countryside again everything came back with even greater intensity. The car was crawling along by this time so as we limped into our street we realised that the short journey had taken over two and a half hours and it was three in the morning. As we got out of the car the 'Presence' came with us, into our small terraced house, right into the living room and kitchen amongst the ordinariness of our belongings. We seemingly could not escape. We 'humanist, vegetarian, environmentalist' know-it-alls simply did not know what to do. I asked John what we should do so he suggested ringing our recent hosts. It showed the measure of our terror that we could even think of ringing someone up at that mad hour, but there was no choice.

The phone rang out for a long time. This was long before the days of mobile phones and they were obviously asleep in a room without an extension. A very sleepy voice answered and, apologising profusely, I shakily explained to Fliss what was happening. She just gasped in amazement and seemed speechless. When I asked her what we could do she said, 'I suggest you pray'.

Prayer had been easy for me throughout my traumatic childhood and during those teenage years when I was looking for God but I had not attempted it for ten years. I don't think John ever had, but we both knelt down and I asked Jesus to come and mediate between us and this terrifying Being who had invaded our lives. Exhausted we fell into bed and slept like new-born babes, all three of us.

In the morning Chris and Fliss rang to say they were going to drive over to see us, that they could only stay a few minutes but wanted to see us after the events of the night before. We thought it very strange that they should take the trouble to come all that way for a minute or two but were delighted to see them. They brought us a Bible – the Good News version – and sped away after lots of hugs and not a few tears. Again, we did not know what all the fuss was about but after they had gone I opened this unfamiliar book which just happened to open at the story of Easter. I read how Jesus had died, been buried and had risen again and that He was still alive and for the first time in my life I knew it was true. I just knew. He had died for me and because of that I would never die, that one day I would go to Heaven to be with Him forever!! There was no need for anyone to tell me. I knew. For absolute certain. I also knew that God was close to me and always had been.

The excitement I felt was so overpowering that I am not sure if I assumed that John was going through the same experience or he actually was. Hindsight is a great thing, isn't it? At the time he seemed to be in exactly the same place as I was, indeed for years that seemed to be the case. It was only much later that I began to doubt this to be true. Of course, he says now that he made it all up but I am not sure. Only the Lord knows and one day it will be clear to me as well but I firmly believed at the time that he too was seeing the world in a completely new and different way and his life certainly changed dramatically.

In fact, everything changed overnight. On the following Sunday Chris and Felicity took us to St Michael Le Belfry in York where the Vicar David Watson had been ministering for a few years to a very large student congregation. The Sunday evening service was entirely given over to reaching out to this population and, outside the building as we approached, wonderful Israeli music was playing as girls danced around in huge circles resembling Greek dancing. Inside, the large traditional church building was buzzing.

Many people brought friends along to hear the good news of Jesus (which we had just experienced first-hand!) and the pews quickly filled up.

I remember little of the service, except that the music was amazing and that there was a drama group which did a wonderful little presentation, but when David Watson got up to speak I was immediately hooked. His message was the same message as the one we had heard the previous week at the Lane's house and his appeal for those who wanted to accept Jesus Christ's gift of new life to come out to the front had me out there like a shot. I prayed the prayer which David recited for us, alongside many others, just in case I had got it wrong the other night, and sat down absolutely sure that I was now a Christian. Maybe it should have rung warning bells when John did not go out to the front, but I simply put that down to our different personalities at the time.

All I knew was that this holy and very present person, the God of the Bible, had come to me and was speaking to me very clearly and I was in constant conversation with Him. He seemed to be everywhere, in every moment, more real than anything in my life had ever been and completely apparent: in the trees, the stars, the wind and rain. And He cared about me and the concerns that I had! This awesome, mighty, Holy Person cared about me!

One of my first concerns was my little boy who, although very small, would one day grow up and I was so desperate to know that he too would be saved. The Lord gave me a scripture to hold onto the first week after my conversion; He told me that He would save my children.

"I will contend with those who contend with you, and your children I will save." Isaiah 49 v 25b

The verse that He gave me talks of children and actually translates properly as offspring. Now that I have many more offspring, including children, grandchildren and at time of writing one great grandchild, I find myself praying for many more to come to Christ. He says that He will do this and over the years I have had to believe this and pray and wait for all of them to be saved, sometimes with great faith and assurance, and at other times in desperation and weariness, but always in the hope that they will all be His one day.

As for John and I, we knew nothing of what it meant to be Christians, true believers, and had no pre-conceived ideas about what to do next. That was not necessary though as the Lord was in charge now and He did! John's parents were away on holiday for the next two weeks and we were 'house sitting'. This entailed a long walk down a quiet country lane as the last bit of my half-hour stroll from town. Pushing the pram (coachbuilt in those days and very heavy) all the way back with the shopping underneath and Isaac asleep inside, I passed by a house I would not normally have seen if we were in our own home.

At the bottom of the garden, right next to the road, was a large post and on the top was a sign. This was strange enough in itself but on the sign was painted in large letters for all to see 'Is God Reaching out to you?' I nearly fell over with surprise but immediately turned the pram into the drive, walked up to the front door and knocked loudly. A young woman wearing an apron and obviously busy with her housework opened the door and I blurted out, 'Yes! I know God is reaching out to me.'

Barry and Joan were a very young couple with two small boys who had come to live in our small Yorkshire town to set up a church. His father was a pastor of a church in a nearby town and that group had sent the couple to start a new work and lead their own church. Barry was amazed as I described to them both what had happened the week before and could not wait to meet John and invite us to the meetings which they had started only a few months before. These took place in the waiting room of a dentist who had joined with Barry in leading the group and consisted of only a dozen or so people.

When they heard that we were musicians this enthusiastic pair were delighted – they had been praying for worship leaders (we had no idea what that meant) and therefore we seemed to be the answer. Within a few weeks we had become active members of their group and were all set to sing at a large meeting in a nearby town when I mentioned we were not married. Worse still, I told them that I was still married to Clive and they were horrified. So far were we from God's ways that we didn't even think this was a problem. Needless to say, we did not sing and could not be baptised until my divorce was through but the elders of the church decided we could stay together because of Isaac – we were already a family and should not be separated. This created problems for some members of the group and looking back I wonder if that was a mistake. However, I have found that looking back with the light I have now on mistakes in my earlier years walking with the Lord is a pointless and sometimes depressing activity! As new baby believers with no real idea about God's ways and with our very damaged consciences through years of sin, we just did what the church leaders told us to do.

Very soon, however, we were married and became active members of the church, baptised with great joy and able to lead worship and minister in song together. We planned to have another child to complete our little family. We were both seemingly changing as we grew in faith. God was very real to me and we were happy with our new life. Wonderfully I discovered that the love I had for Isaac was deep and enduring and I was not afraid of being a terrible mother any more. My past experiences did not need to poison my relationship with my children and he was a delightful, bright and happy little boy. John became involved in a Christian band, developing into a wonderful father to Isaac, who adored him, and my relationship with Mum improved greatly when she gave her life to the Lord. Sadly though, the marriage was not at all what I had imagined it would be when we had committed our lives to the Lord and to each other and there were many issues from our past which were to threaten to overwhelm me and rob us of this happiness.

We had brought into our marriage and our Christian life the sins we had done and the sins which had been committed against us. Of course, everything which is outside of God's perfect plan is sin but there are some things which poison and pollute us more than others. I can't speak for John but I am sure that this 'baggage' we both carried was so heavy that, if not doomed, our relationship was a ship pretty well scuppered from the start. Perhaps we needed to be apart or perhaps we both clung to the past rather than letting go of those mistakes, allowing God to heal and cleanse.

I remember a dream I had at some point early in our relationship. In the house where we were first together the staircase was enclosed by a door on the ground floor. In the dream someone had opened up the staircase to reveal the area below it and I could see deep into the foundations which were completely rotten; just like the foundations of our relationship they would need to be ripped out and completely rebuilt or the house would eventually come crashing down around our heads. Unfortunately, the foundations of our relationship were never renewed.

So, two weddings had happened, there had been a ‘funeral’ of sorts of my old life when I surrendered to Jesus, going joyfully through the waters of baptism. However, if I thought that this meant the new life which God had given to me would be easy I was very much mistaken. He had given me a second chance but now the real work would begin.

6. Old Wounds Leave Scars

I have come to the conclusion that I am a slow learner, or at least it seems to me that it has taken God many years to teach me the valuable lessons which have transformed my life. Perhaps it is more that I am, like so many, too quick to forget. Jewish tradition says that something is only learnt when it is truly applied to one's life, lived out in daily experience, not just pontificated about in study halls. I have come to see that this is the way the Lord works. We can know something, really believe it, memorise it – storing it as knowledge – but we only really know it when it has been worked through in our experience and tried and tested in the furnace of life on this planet. Even then we may need to repeat the lesson for it to permanently endure.

We live in a fallen and corrupt world but the Lord will use the experiences of life, both past and present, within that environment to show us how much we need to change. He will subsequently use His Word to teach us how to change if we allow Him to do so. Only by staying close to Him can we actually make any progress and He will slowly and painstakingly work with us to make sure that we become the people He created us to be. This takes time. There are no quick fixes. There are, however, real milestones of change which are those points when true growth and change happen and when real healing takes place. By His Grace there were to be many of these in the years to come.

Jesus said when speaking about the woman who washed his feet with her tears and dried them with her hair that those who have been forgiven much love much. I was a woman taken in adultery and destined for destruction so my love for Him is immense. It has taken over forty years for me to really begin to see how great His love is for me. In fact, I wrote a song many years ago which says it very clearly. The chorus goes: 'If you don't know it by now, with all that I've given to you. If you don't know it by now then you'll never know my great love for you.' Fortunately for me God is patient with those who follow Him. He has been mercifully patient with me.

Life after new-birth did not become a bed of roses just because I had met the Lord – far from it. In the early, heady days of this new life in Christ everything seemed bright, clear and fairly easy. I think this is like a 'honeymoon period' that the Lord gives His spiritual babes when they first come into this new Kingdom, which is so different from the world from which He has rescued us. We are indeed like new–born babies, craving milk, not able to walk and actually needing to be carried around to even survive. However, once we have learnt to take our first baby steps, He begins to stretch us, gently at first, and then more robustly as he expects us to begin to grow that new spiritual life within. Of course, the old, not-so-spiritual life (what the Bible calls the 'flesh life') is constantly calling us, threatening to trip us up as we set off on this new walk.

Some of us come into this life carrying some pretty hefty baggage from the past and we were no exception. I can't really go into John's – that is his story – but there were definitely things from his life before our encounter with Jesus

As for me, as we have seen in the early part of this book, there was much imprinted on my heart which was ugly and painful; consequently, it was certain that the scars from the past were not going to disappear overnight. Some of them obviously were self-inflicted – I had made some disastrously bad decisions in the ten years after I said no to the Lord, but that which had been done to me as a young child had left its mark. Was I going to carry all of this throughout my life on Earth or was there really going to be freedom from the past?

God gave me a promise right at the beginning of my journey with Him that he was going to restore my life, heal those scars and the trauma and pain which they had left, but I had no idea how, or how deeply buried some of them were. I saw myself as a real mess, had very little self-esteem and the self-worth of a gnat. One of God's first promises to me was that He would heal me, then He would heal my land. He told me that I was His beautiful English Rose and that he was going to restore my life and when He had done so He would restore my England. There would be a great spiritual awakening here and I would witness it.

Wonderfully the Creator of the Universe was speaking to me. Prayer was so real and a two-way communication. He was reaching out to me all the time, telling me of His love for me and this broken world. He also began to show me some of the issues which were strangling my heart and making it impossible for me to draw closer to Him.

I suppose the thing which had most impacted on all my relationships was the rejection and fear which I carried around wherever I went. Always I was afraid that if I loved anyone they would ultimately leave me alone because I truly believed that I was unlovable. This meant that even if they stayed they really did not want to be with me. Why would they? Those who may have wanted to be my friends I viewed with suspicion and mistrust and questioned their motives, ultimately expecting betrayal and hurt.

This heavy load made it impossible for me to see anyone's real feelings towards me, made me sure that people were against me, that they would eventually leave me on my own. This even reflected on my sense of God's opinion of and relationship with me. I was convinced that I needed to earn His favour to keep His love or even He would leave me, rejecting me like everyone else. I was jealous and paranoid and sure that all my new-found Christian friends were not genuine and that all of them were talking about me or laughing at me. This intense negativity affected all who came close to me except my children. As the others were born, I only became surer of their love for me but of course that was because they were my children. I reasoned that they had no choice but to love me because they were dependent on me. Also, I could relate to children far better than adults. Perhaps this was because deep in my heart I was still a child and because of my childish emotions children were the only ones with whom I could find any real connection.

Added to my lack of trust were John's own problems which were buried as deeply as my own. He was not in touch with his feelings at all and, apart from the band members, he had not formed any real relationships in the church either. Although he was heavily involved with the band when they moved to Sheffield, a year after our conversion, they did not take him with them, finding instead a local guitarist to fill his role. It was at this point that his mood changed, making him more likely to miss church meetings or avoid Christians in general. He seemed to become more irritable, sometimes losing his temper completely – usually with me if I became emotional – and I often felt that I was walking on eggshells.

I too was still struggling with my own issues. Although we were singing together and had begun to write worship songs together I was constantly suspicious and jealous of other women (despite the fact that he was a great dad). I was unable to see myself as lovable and therefore loved. Even if he had once loved me John would have found it very hard to take and I guess he went looking for someone who would appreciate him. Also, I was weighed down with exhaustion from broken nights and looking after the children and too many pregnancies too close together. After a few years of this and having to contend with my mother also who had come to live with us in Harrogate, things were looking dire when we were sent to a Midlands conurbation to set up the local branch of an international Christian charity.

Living with my mother had proved toxic for our tattered relationship. She had needed to come to us as her mental health problems were growing. She had come to Christ herself during the stay, which was wonderful, but her dislike for John grew all the more apparent. She complained about him constantly and in the end I could see no good in him either. When we went to live in the Midlands she was supposed to follow once the house was sold, but she met up with an old friend from home and was going to get married, miraculously. We would have a fresh start.

The church which had sponsored the youth and community worker was an Anglican institution in which we both found it difficult to settle. Eventually John had stopped going to church altogether and for a while I began to drift with him, putting my relationship with God on the back burner in an attempt to save our marriage.

Things did improve and John's outburst of anger and frustration with his lot seemed to abate as he got involved in this new project. I was too tired and ill much of the time to really be much help but things were beginning to take off when our fourth child, Jacob, was born. We had become members of a Baptist church where John felt at home; he was involved with the youth work and we made some new friends.

Slowly however I became aware that the minister had some very strange ideas, most of which were not in the Bible. In this man's view the Bible was not meant to be taken literally and he had some strange views about Jesus and His miracles. Such incidents as walking on water were explained away by hidden sand banks, the feeding of the five thousand miracle was simply a case of everyone sharing their packed lunch. This minister of the gospel actually believed that Jesus died because God could not save Him, that everyone was going to Heaven anyway so the sacrifice of Christ on the cross to pay for our sin was not necessary. His teaching was so far from biblical truth that I began to wonder if in fact I was wrong and the Bible was not meant to be taken literally. This was especially strong a pull as John was quite happy with these liberal ideas and with this Baptist church. As a relatively new believer I was confused and often found myself doubting my own convictions and trust in the word of God. I became more and more unhappy and emotionally unstable as my whole world in Jesus began to shake.

This came to a head the evening that the minister came round to talk to us about having Jacob dedicated. He did his duty as pastor of the church and took us through the ceremony, which was planned for the following week.

When he had finished, I could not stop myself from asking him what the purpose of this was; if the Bible was not to be believed then what was the spiritual dimension of this event anyway? He really could not answer me but both he and John became impatient with my questions and the meeting ended with many issues unresolved. After he left John and I continued to talk and, eventually beginning to be swayed to their point of view, I said, 'Maybe we aren't supposed to believe this book literally!' picking up my Bible from the kitchen table. John was standing by the sink and the very next words that came out of his mouth stunned and appalled me. ‘I am leaving you,’ he said. ‘I don’t love you and I don’t want to be married anymore.’

Between us there was a strip of floor around six feet wide; it was a big kitchen, and as he spoke I had a vision of a huge black hole opening up in the floor between us and I literally saw the enormous gulf that there was between us. It was as if when I uttered those words of doubt in His Word the Lord said ‘So far and no further’. Between them John and our church leader – my husband and my pastor who were in spiritual authority in my life – were destroying my faith and God would not allow it to go any further. Jacob was just nine weeks old at the time but it took his daddy a year to actually leave us.

I did not know it at the time but this was to be the turning point in my walk with God that was to bring me closer to Him than ever before. Now was to really begin the transformation in my life which would unlock the chains which still tied me to the past, allowing me to be really free in Him. Although it was without doubt one of the most difficult times I have had to walk through with the Lord it was a necessary valley if I was to know the depth of His love for me. This had to happen if I was to really know Him as my Father God, know who I was in Christ and be of any use in His service. As Charles Dickens says in *A Tale of Two Cities*, “It was the best of times; it was the worst of times.”

7. A lone parent but not alone

It is January again and a year since I started this memoir! Already so much has happened this year that I cannot begin to imagine how much of the last forty-something years to include in this account. It must be said that everything that we go through has a purpose in God's economy but not all of it can be included here. Shall we say that, just as the glimpses from the early years of my life and the earliest years of my new life in Christ were the lowlights and the highlights of the first half of my sojourn on this planet, so the next part of my story is really just that: a selection of the events through which He has taken me since I found myself a lone parent, but never alone.

As has already been said, life had not become a bed of roses because I had met the Lord – far from it. The difference was that those difficulties through which I was going now and would go through in the future had purpose and could be used by Him to bring me nearer to the place where He wanted me to be. Sometimes I was not aware of this but eventually I would see that the truth of Romans 8 verse 28 is simply that. Everything does work for good for those who are His because He works everything together for that purpose and for His glory.

The following year was horrible as I was left to bring up the children on my own for so much of the time and struggle with the knowledge that their father was planning his exit from our lives. We were a little unit – the kids and I did everything almost as if we were a single-parent family already. John was so often at work or away, immersing himself in the charity and becoming a complete workaholic. He played the part well of a Christian worker but we rarely saw him and our relationship was pretty non-existent. This time was the beginning of my single-parent role but the difference was that the children did not know their father's plans or thoughts. They were, as much as I could possibly manage, protected from the reality of our dying marriage.

God had moved me to another fellowship after a good friend found me sobbing in the children's playroom one day and asked me if I should leave the Baptist church which had given such terrible teaching to us both. I asked John, who by this time had stopped going anyway, and as he said he didn't care (he didn't much care about anything we did by this time) I prayed for the right spiritual home for me and the children. The Lord took me to Scripture once again and the story of the young prince Joash in Kings... He was going to put us into the care of the Elders of Israel.

In this story the nasty queen Athaliah was intent on murdering the young prince as he was a threat to her hold on the throne, but he was safely hidden in the Temple under the care of the elders. God spoke clearly to me that I should move to a central Evangelical church where the elders there would care for us and keep us safe while we were in this difficult position. A woman alone with four small children is very vulnerable and I was emotionally and mentally a mess. My spiritual life was also in tatters after the awful teaching of the liberal pastor and his congregation. Physically worn out with all the work involved with looking after my family I needed the strength of a Bible-believing church around me and that is certainly what I got.

After almost a year of the terrible uncertainty of living with a husband who wanted to leave us things came to a head. John had applied for a job with the same charity in London, telling me that if he got it he would leave us and if he did not he would stay. A bit of a lottery really but also a bit of a relief. I had actually sat him down one day, not too long before he announced his intention to use this 'throw of the dice' to choose our future, asking him to make up his mind. One minute he was leaving, the next he loved me and was staying. I was losing my sanity slowly and we were all living on a knife edge. Of course, I kept this from my precious children, after all I was a consummate actress, so practised in wearing my mask that I put it on daily just to leave the house, such was my constant level of anxiety.

The day he took the phone call accepting the job I ran from the room sobbing and he came after me with a real anger that my crying might cost him the job. I cried out to the Lord for help which stopped him in his tracks. Instead of the initial anger he became distraught, breaking down in sobs himself. I saw then that he was trapped in his desire to escape his life with us and unable to stop himself from going. Maybe he was having a breakdown and would come back to us restored and healed. At that time I did not know he was already involved with someone else as he had always sworn to me that there was no-one.

On July 26th 1985 John went to a conference in Europe as a delegate and never came back. I was now really alone with four young children – Jacob was one, Roxy was exactly four that day, Caleb five and Isaac was seven. He left after our sweet little four-year-old's birthday party had finished, as I was bathing Jacob, and I still remember crying in the bathroom causing the little birthday girl to go and call her big brothers to help Mummy because I was so upset and couldn't tell them why.

I knew John had found himself an apartment but he didn't tell the children he was never coming back and for two weeks I agonised over this, until it became obvious that I had to tell them. Jacob was too little to understand, the two middle ones were confused but Isaac knew what this meant and was inconsolable. I don't think John ever believed me when I told him the devastating effect this event had on all of them at different times over the next few years. This was me 'being vindictive' and 'unreasonable' but in truth they suffered far more than I did. Indeed, after the first few weeks I experienced a great sense of relief and freedom I had never known and was happier than I could believe. Escaping the claustrophobic and traumatic life we had shared was like stepping out of a cage and for the first time in my life I felt safe. Now the truth of God's Word really came home to me as He really was a husband to the widow and a father to the fatherless and in every way He cared for us and provided for us. My only real anguish was watching my children's distress as they faithfully prayed for their father's return to us for the next two years.

My mother had by this time remarried, re-settling up in the north-west with my step-father; John's mum and dad still lived in Yorkshire. His parents were very shocked by him leaving us and I think Mum felt vindicated as she had always mistrusted and disliked him. Both sets of grandparents were at a loss really because, although they wanted to help me, they were unable to be practically supportive because of the distances between us. A week after his departure they came up with a 'solution' to what they perceived as my unbearable burden. They had got together and decided they would share this by concocting a clever plan.

My mother rang me a few weeks after John left to say that she and dear George, my step-father, would take my little girl and bring Roxy up for me in Lancashire. The in-laws would take my baby boy and Jacob would live in Yorkshire with them so that I would just have Caleb and Isaac to look after. So not only had I lost a husband I was to give up two of my precious children and allow them to be brought up by two sets of grandparents, neither of which were to be anywhere near to those two boys, or to me.

This was not a solution I even considered for a second. Actually, I was appalled at the time that this was the only way they could see to support me but I guess they were afraid that I would not be able to cope at all, afraid that then the children would be taken away by social services – a much worse scenario! And, of course, they were right. There was no way that I could have coped alone. But I was not alone.

Not long after John came back from the conference to our home town, temporarily living alone in his flat before his move to London, I came very close to taking the four children round for him to look after. This was the morning after I had been awake all night with them all in bed with me as they, and I, had all contracted chickenpox. Ill, exhausted, at around five a.m. I rang my pastor's house and told his wife Pat what I was planning. Thankfully, she talked me out of it, wise lady, pointing out that I would not want my children to be in the care of a man who would walk out on us. The tiredness abated a little, the illness passed quite quickly, and the panic that I would not cope faded for the time being.

Although life was far from pleasant, in very real ways I was never alone. The church where God had planted us supported me during this period and the Lord Himself was with me in a way that I had never experienced before. His Word promises that He will not test us beyond what we can endure and this is true. Although I came pretty close to the edge sometimes, He was always there, keeping me from falling.

One picture which had stuck in my mind was when Jacob took his first steps. This, as any parent will tell you, is a pivotal moment in your child's life and one which all parents cherish forever. I can still see little Jakey, my pet name for him still, tottering across our large kitchen/dining room as I stood by the cooker, still smell the macaroni cheese bubbling in the oven and almost hear the Lord say to me, 'Aww look!' It was as if Jesus was in the room with me, His arm around me, gazing like a doting father at His son's first steps. Throughout this period of being a single parent His presence was so real that Jacob as a young child said he had two daddies, the one he cried for every time John dropped him off after a visit, and Jesus who stayed with him always.

Financially things were bad but God always met all our needs and during this time I truly was looked after by Him and His people. Now I was alone with the children I felt God's presence in a tangible way and He was able to begin to show me His love for me in practical and emotional support the way a husband should. God promises to be a father to the fatherless and a husband to the widow and He really is. I was not fully able to really appreciate this though and I knew there was much more that He needed to do in my life. At last I was to begin to let go of the past and let Him heal me. This care from my Heavenly Father was despite the fact that in a very real sense I had brought the whole situation upon myself. The children too were suffering because of my past sin; the sins of the fathers really are visited on the children. I knew that God had forgiven me because I had trusted Jesus as my Saviour but He could not eradicate all the results of that sin. My poor offspring were paying the price of my and their father's mistakes as God worked out His purposes in our lives. His mercy for us, His great compassion, meant that we were not going to be destroyed by this; He was preparing restoration.

Now I know that this was where my real life in Christ properly began because up until the day John left us I was tied to him. Whether he was a believer who had walked away from the Lord or a non-Christian the whole time who had sought to be part of something he had only witnessed from the outside but never experienced for himself, I still do not know, but that is immaterial. When I was with him I could not truly and unequivocally live for Jesus as John was always pulling me back and I really believe God was giving him as much time as was possible to turn around and follow Him. When this began to damage my faith the Lord said enough and took him away; even the elders had noticed that the children were more settled once their father had left the home and told me that the Lord had taken him away so He could 'sort him out'. The thing about God is, though, even He can't 'sort us out' if we don't want to be, if we don't want to change!

Now the Lord drew me closer to Himself and, through the presence of His Holy Spirit and the wonderful Bible-believing Church I was now part of, He began to restore the years which had been spoiled. He was making me into the woman He had created me to be and this was going to take a lot of work. Progressive sanctification the Bible teachers call it; to me it is simply just making me the person He intended me to be, set apart for Him alone, completely His. First though I had to get honest with God.

Have you ever yelled at the Lord? Really shouted out in rage at the Lord of all creation? The Bible says 'Be angry with God and do not sin' so that means it is allowed. I did not dare however tell God what I in truth thought about my grotty life and the way I had been treated by everyone who was supposed to nurture and protect me. The thing is He already knew better than I did how I was feeling. He was not at all fooled by my nice words and set smiles. He wanted me to be real with him in order that I could be honest with myself but I could not do it ... until I met an evangelist called David who came to Burton about a year after my family had been torn apart.

This man told me to be honest with the Lord and quoted Job 10 as an example. In verses 18 and 19 Job, who has a pretty awful experience where all his children die, all his riches disappear and he is covered in sores, says this to the Almighty:

"Why then did you bring me out of the womb? I wish I had died before any eye saw me. If only I had never come into being, or had been carried straight from the womb to the grave!" Job 10 vs 18 - 19

Wow! It seemed that thousands of years ago this man from ancient history had been reading my mind. Job knew exactly how I felt and had got away with telling God all about his feelings in a very direct, almost brutal way. The next Saturday when the children went off for the day with their dad I decided I would let God have it – both barrels

I went into my bedroom to cry out my complaints, and it really was a very long, agonising list of woes. I cried and shouted and screamed at God, asking Him that if He knew that all this list of horrible happenings was going to happen to me why did He allow me to be born in the first place. Why let me be born into that hellish family and live with those two women who hated each other? Why give me a father who rejected and abandoned me and refused to even acknowledge my existence by sending me a single birthday card? Why leave me to the mercy of Godfrey and all the other men who had taken advantage of my spoiled and soiled womanhood?

If He knew this – as He must have done because He is outside of time and knows everything anyway – why let me live to inherit a life which was such a mess where I was unable to make any meaningful connections with people work? A life where I seemed therefore destined to repeat those mistakes again and again, only to end up alone and in despair? Destined to do to Clive what my dad had done to my mother. Destined to live with and then marry a man who did not love me, who would leave me and our children, consigning them to a fatherless world like mine. Why? Why? Why?

I sobbed and shouted and screamed from the depths of my being, the anguish of my soul, until I was all cried out and completely spent. A great peace descended on me which was full of a great silence as time seemed to stand still in my room, in the universe. Then, in that silence, I heard a deep, still voice in my heart. God spoke just four words, 'Because I love you'. This broke me totally.

God loves us – He just loves us. We are his children, His delight, and His pleasure. In the thirty-odd years since that afternoon in Needwood Street He has spent every moment of my life showing me this love. Although at first I did not realise it that day I had only just scratched the surface of its depths; in fact, I know that I still have only understood a tiny fraction of the great ocean of the love of God. Nevertheless, He began to show me (and of course He continues to do so) the depth and height and breadth of this love and I increasingly learn how to recognise that every detail of His plan for my life proves it.

8. Love your neighbour as yourself

Have you ever struggled with that command? Have you ever thought that it was impossible to accept, comfort, care for others the way that you do yourself? This is I think fairly understandable because at our very centre we are inherently selfish. However, my problem was slightly different. When I first really heard this command, really heard it for myself like a bolt out of the blue, not many weeks after I had become a Christian, it became to me a dilemma. At that time I realised that rather than loving myself I did not like myself; in fact there were definitely times when even after I had met the Lord I hated myself. How could I love others as myself when there was no love there for myself?

This is probably why I was attracted to men who would let me down or even potentially mistreat me. To my mind this was all I deserved in fact and fulfilled the self-fulfilling prophecy that I always believed. Men would always let you down – after all they always had. My life was not worth very much, so why would people treat me well, or if they did, they most definitely had an ulterior motive. I was myself a great manipulator, only really interested in turning situations or people to my own advantage. I was a complete control freak because my life was so full of fear. Having been for the majority of my life a user of others I expected to be used.

One solitary exception was that I had such great love for my children; this was a wonderful new experience for me – sacrificial love which wanted only the best for someone. I saw this as a transforming gift from God as soon as I was born again because the motherly love we are supposed to have when our children pop into this world had passed me by initially. This was partly due to Mum's inability to show her love for me, although I came to see that she could not help this. I also came to see that she always loved me even when she was totally incapable of expressing it by any other means than giving me money.

Isaac my first-born, then Caleb two years later, became the centre of my life; everything about them delighted me, making me increasingly sure that motherhood was my best role so far. They were like chalk and cheese: Isaac constantly needing stimulus through books; Caleb a calm, happy little chap with a seemingly quiet nature who loved his big brother totally. When my beautiful daughter, Roxy, came along life had been hard but she was so wonderful it completely compensated me for all the anguish of my other failing relationships. I had actually wondered if I could love a girl after my disastrous relationship with my mum. I need not have worried; she was and always will be my delight. Jacob, my baby, still fills me with tender thoughts as an adult as only youngest children can. Such a delightful baby boy, he always will.

When it came to loving me however it was a different matter. For one thing I knew how horrible I was and I had no self-esteem or feeling of self- worth. In fact, many times I was still being almost overwhelmed by those suicidal thoughts and feelings which almost ended my life in my teens. I firmly believed that if people – especially all the wonderful new friends I had made in the church – knew what the real me was really like they would reject me, just as my dad had done and just as I regularly did myself. Besides which I had grown so used to wearing my protective covering just to be able to function in the world I was not even aware that it was there most of time. Therefore, letting anyone get close enough to know me properly was not an option; I just did not realise it. Perhaps this was one of the reasons that John had become so increasingly distant and eventually left altogether to find someone else. I saw myself as having failed again in this marriage and did not blame him in the end.

As a child I had lived in a fantasy world into which I would retreat whenever I was lonely or afraid, which was most of the time. As an adult I had learnt to perform in order to play the part I thought people wanted so, naturally, as a Christian I had tried to continue to hide much of my real self so that I would be safe and, most importantly, be accepted in the church. Worst of all, I told myself that even God was bound to reject me when He finally found out what a hopeless case I was and realised how little I trusted Him. Ridiculous as it might sound, back then I still thought I could hide from Him! Outwardly I might seem happy and confident but inside there were still times of great anxiety, jealousy, suspicion and downright lack of trust. But I was not going to admit this to myself or to my Heavenly Father – and because I had to be strong to survive as a single parent my children were not going to see me weak if at all possible.

Sadly, by living behind my protective shell I set impossibly high standards for myself. Perfectionism always leads one to feel a failure but for a Christian there is even more reason not to be trapped in this. It was impossible for the Lord to give me His strength if I was pretending that I could cope. The problem was I still feared the men in the white coats would come and take me away if I lost control of my feelings and my sanity would be lost forever. Nana had done a really good job on me!

My grandmother's warning that they would 'see what the doctor can do with you' if I did not behave still haunted me. Also, I wanted to please the Lord so much so that He would not leave me and because I knew how much I had been forgiven and I loved Him for that. The problem with that was how could He give me His new life if I was trying so hard to be 'a good girl' so 'Daddy God' would not leave me? Finally, there was the ever-present spectre of the social services team coming to take my precious children away if I did crack up. This could never be allowed to happen.

It was not surprising that I was so weak emotionally after John left, as well as feeling vulnerable in every way. The children's distress was far worse than my situation as I felt better in many ways than I had for years. No need to tread carefully anymore; free to become as involved as I wanted to in the church without worrying about upsetting anyone. I had borne the major role in caring for the children for a while as his job became more and more consuming but being in sole charge of four small children is extremely stressful, which took its toll on my sleep patterns. My mind just would not switch off so I went to the doctor for help as poor sleep was making me totally exhausted and I could not relax at all. Remember, I was a single parent with four small children, a fact that seemed to escape the GP who prescribed something quite strong to aid my sleeping. In the morning after my first real night's sleep for weeks Caleb came to me and said he had tried to wake me up during the night and could not. He was being sick at the time. I realised then that the doctor was very unwise; to keep my children safe I could not take the medication

Later that day I was reading my Bible. As I read the account of the paralysed man who could not get into the healing waters at Siloam the Lord spoke to me, 'Do you want to be healed?' Jesus had asked that man the same question and I wasn't about to start making the same excuses that he had. 'Yes, I do,' I told Him and He said 'Then you are.' Immediately I knew that I was. The constant stream of thoughts which had befuddled my mind since John left, keeping me from sleep and any kind of rest, stopped suddenly and I was able to totally relax for the first time in years.

With His help the children and I survived for the next few years, but God says that we are 'more than conquerors'. He does not want us to just survive. He wants us to soar like eagles above the storms which inevitably come in this fallen world in which we live. He was about to show His compassion to me in a really tangible way. Into this confused and broken family God sent a gift that was to help with the healing and transformation which He was intent on doing in my life – the gift of unconditional love which was to show me for the first time that I was in fact lovable. It was to enable me in due time to be able to feel loved by people and, more wonderful still, to experience the love of God which I had accepted but had known only by faith and in theory. Although I had been a Christian for seven years I had never felt this.

This gift was not only for me but also for my precious children; I longed for them to grow up in a family of two parents who loved them and would care for them together as they developed into young people and adults.

This gift was to come through a very ordinary human being because of the transforming grace of the King of Kings. This gift was Dan.

9. Together - Forever

Have you ever wondered if there was any use moving on, going forward or even indeed living at all? Did you ever think that the world, your family/friends and especially you would be better off if you just weren't here?

Has that terrible thought and the following awful words ever come through your mind and out of your mouth 'I wish I was dead!'? Or have you even attempted to end your life believing that this would put everyone out of their misery once and for all?

If the answer to any or all of the above is a yes, however tentative or positive, then you are reading the right book. You are the reason I have been sitting here for months (probably years by now) looking out of my dining room window in all weathers and writing this account. This is for you if your life seems to have been lived for the most part in a black hole or a long dark tunnel and even though you might be able to at last see the light at the end of the tunnel you are not sure yet if you will ever fully emerge. Let me tell you right now on this chilly March afternoon that if you put your hand in the hand of God – or indeed if you have already – and keep on walking with Him you will come out of the darkness into this beautiful garden where all the promises He has made to man are yours for the whole of eternity.

This all began for me when I first met the Lord on that amazing night in my car but I would be lying if I said that it was all plain sailing from then on – quite the opposite. It was soon clear that I had brought a lot of stuff with me into this kingdom of light and life and some of it was very dark indeed. What became clear to me however was that Jesus was walking with me through the darkness, even though sometimes I could not see Him. Sometimes, in the darkest of nights however He would make His glorious presence known.

One incident truly shines out as a miraculous intervention and it all began when Jacob lost the backdoor keys.

We often lived in one of the downstairs rooms, an enormous kitchen/dining room in which a three-piece suite fitted comfortable. We all slept together in one of the bedrooms – I just could simply not afford to heat the whole house. It had been bought as an investment when we moved to the Midlands as we expected that John would eventually work in London. He was on the up-and-up with the Christian charity that he worked for until he left us, so we believed we would be able to sell this and buy a tiny property near the capital. Obviously when he did eventually go to work in the capital we were not asked to accompany him.

Jacob was only a toddler, mischievous, with a curious streak, who would love to play with the bunch of keys which dangled from the backdoor. One day he hid them somewhere as a game. The problem was he could not remember where he had put them and I could not find them as I desperately searched the whole house. A very dear couple from the church came round to try to help with this crisis and while Barbara and I had a cuppa her husband, Jim, tried to sort this problem out. Unfortunately, he decided, after trying to solve this problem for ages, there was only one thing for it – a new lock, which he would come to fit the next day.

That meant being in the great rambling old vicarage overnight with four small children on my own (nothing new there) but with the backdoor unlocked. This was a real problem as we had often had people try to climb over the back gate to invade our large back garden while I had been alone. This meant that I was especially nervous. This was before we got our large soppy but ferocious-sounding black Labrador, Gip, and his naughty whippet-cross sidekick, Pippy, who would successfully see off any and all real or imaginary intruders.

In the huge dining/kitchen/living room at the back of the house we had an old battered three-piece suite, several dining chairs and a heavy old wooden table. Along with any toy boxes or stools, I proceeded to pile every bit of furniture up against the back door which, thankfully, opened inwards. It must have looked comical – and indeed I might have found it hilarious at any other time – but I simply found it a reassuring obstacle for any potential home invader.

That evening I did manage to relax enough to go and sit in the front room after putting the kids to bed and as I sat praying – probably for God's protection – I had the strangest sensation.

I suddenly became aware of being watched by unseen eyes, all around me. I could see nothing but the faded wallpaper and the furniture, yet I was sure that I was completely surrounded. Incredibly I was not afraid, not just not afraid of these 'watchers' but not afraid at all. Not afraid of the night time in a house with no locked back door. That night I slept soundly and when we all woke up and went downstairs the house was as I had left it – piled up furniture included.

Later in the morning when Jim and Barbara returned, Jim busied himself with the new lock and Barbara told me of her relief to find us unscathed, following a sound, untroubled night's sleep. She had been very worried about us and when she returned home had been praying for our safety. When I told her about my experience the night before she was absolutely amazed. In her prayers for us the previous evening she had been so concerned that she had asked God to surround us with His angels and that I would know that they were all around us.

I certainly did and when, a few days later, I told my pastor, Denis, he said it was like the story in 2 Kings:17 when Elisha's servant had been afraid of all the enemy forces camped around them. Elisha prayed that God would open his servant's eyes so that he could see the Host of Heaven which surrounded them and which vastly outnumbered the enemy. Once more I had been made aware by the Lord of His wonder-working power and His great love for me, God's unconditional love that I still knew so little about but which He was going to unfold to me over the next three decades. This love which is unfathomably deep, immeasurably wide and colossally high and which is for all people.

Learning to be me

When I met my lovely husband Dan I had very little idea what real, unconditional love was. I am not sure I even realised that God loved me for me – I still thought He would probably ditch me as soon as He realised what I was like (daft really as He knows us all very well) but I still thought I could hide the real, obnoxious me from Him as easily as everyone else. No-one had loved me just for me and I certainly did not love myself so when it became obvious that this man did, I was completely flummoxed.

The weekend we met I was still a single parent, living in poverty, in a huge, decaying, freezing old vicarage with four adorable, but still grieving, young children. Every week their dad would come and take them out and their rapturous little faces when he arrived, late as usual, would give me the strength to let them go with him. Distraught and confused when he brought them back, the three oldest ones would smile bravely for me as they knew that I was suffering too. Jacob, my youngest child, who was still a toddler, however, seemed to go through the worst of the separation trauma and would cry for days. The others would wait a little more patiently for the next treat as they were older but all of them missed their dad immensely. Isaac was the eldest, taking on that role magnificently once he had accepted that his dad had gone. I had once, foolishly, promised him that his Daddy would never leave him when he had expressed his anxiety about this. Shortly after he had gone John took Isaac to stay with him in London during the school holidays but that just made the inevitable final break so much harder. I am not sure he ever truly recovered.

Financially things became hard, especially when John lost his job in London and we were trying to survive on benefits. There was nothing towards the mortgage of course, or the massive cost of running our mansion, and there were no such things as food banks back then. On top of this were the debts that he had left us, of which I had known nothing. We had already nearly lost the house when their dad stopped paying the mortgage as both sales which I had arranged fell through when the buyers tried to drop the price at the last minute. They were trying to take advantage of a woman on her own, but of course I was not alone and had been led by the Lord to take in a lodger to help pay bills. Food parcels from people at church would keep us going week by week and I took to baking for the local sandwich bar to help eke out our income. My darling daughter still reminds me that their clothes came out of 'bags' brought round from well-meaning friends and in fact the dress I wore when I met my Dan came from such a bag.

The only way of avoiding homelessness in the end was by taking in the lodger mentioned above, in much the same way Mum had all those decades before. This young lady's rent paid the mortgage. The local council had refused to house me unless I had the house repossessed, offering only a mother and child hostel for seven weeks, after which we were on our own. I would be on the streets and the children taken into care, which was what their dear grandparents had feared when they had made their suggestion of help.

Although having my lodger Lena in the house did alleviate some of the loneliness of being a single parent I was still aware that bringing up four children was a tough role alone and I longed for someone to talk to and to share the ups and downs of family life. To be honest I also missed the closeness of having someone who was mine, especially at times like Christmas when everyone else was celebrating with their families; this was the loneliest time, coming back from church and the packed pews to a huge house where we were left to celebrate by ourselves.

My really good friend Sonia, who had stood by me through thick and thin and who was always there when I needed a lift or help with the children, sat with me one evening and prayed with me for a husband. The Lord had told me to 'let the unbelieving partner go' and my pastor had in fact counselled me to re-marry, as Paul had told the young widows to do back in the first-century Church. We needed a father in the house and I needed a partner with whom I could walk through this life. I think my faith must have begun to strengthen as I did believe that if I needed a husband God would provide one. He promises to provide all our needs. It is certainly true that it is during really tough times our relationship with the Lord grows, inevitably making our faith stronger.

We had just had some teaching on prayer and the idea was that you need to be specific in prayer and then you will know that God has answered specifically. My experience over the years has been that this is a great aid to faith as specific prayers being answered are much less likely to be explained away as coincidence than vague 'Please bless me' ones. I believed then, as I do now, that if you pray with faith in the will of God, He will grant you your requests, so it was plain that He would do this if it was what the children and I needed. Crucially I was also prepared for Him to say no. I had already told Him that I would stay single and bring them up alone if that was what He really wanted.

There we were, making a list! And what a list! I can still see the gas fire in front of the coffee table glowing in the large front room, feel the anticipation as I took up the pen to compose this important epistle to God. This is what I asked the Lord for: a man who loved God more than anything else in the world, who loved me next and who would help me to bring the children up in the Lord. In addition, I asked for someone who was good with money – I never wanted to be in debt again in my life and never know where the money had gone in the first place. I did not want to be rich, only to have someone who, like me, could make a budget and stick to it!

What a prayer – a believing prayer at that. Little did I know that the organisation which had been instrumental in John's leaving us would be used by God to bring my darling Dan into our lives.

This relief and development charity was once an evangelical organisation which had started life as a Bible study group for drapers' assistants during the 19th century. By the middle of the 20th century it had become little more than an international hostel movement. In the 1980s, however, it went through a kind of renaissance and there was a move to sell off these now redundant buildings, thereby releasing funds which could be invested into youth and community work. This is what had brought us to the Midlands and what had led to the now successful relief and development organisation which is the local branch today. When the kids and I were left alone it was because my ex-husband had got another job with this same charity in London, a job which allowed him pursue his single life with a new-found freedom.

Interestingly, and unknown to me, Dan had volunteered to help at the charity with the new local director who had replaced John. Despite this offer he had never heard from them except to receive an invitation to its centenary celebrations at the local town hall. I had received an invitation to the same evening but turned it down as I knew that my absent husband and his girlfriend would be there. I just could not face them. She had been a volunteer with them and I had invited her to my home once but had not seen her since I discovered that they were together.

The afternoon of the event the director rang me to say that John and his girlfriend were not going to be there after all, imploring me to go. My mum and stepdad were staying for the weekend so I had ready-made babysitters. Without thinking too much I said I would go even though I had nothing to wear and no-one to go with. The event was just around the corner from the ex-vicarage where we still lived, just behind the Town Hall, making it possible for me to walk there. A black bin-bag full of clothes had just arrived from a friend, these bags being our substitute at the time for Primark or in fact any other clothes shop. There was no room in our income for clothes; we barely managed food! In this one was a beautiful blue wrap-over dress which fitted my frame perfectly; I even thought I looked quite acceptable in it, so I had no excuse to say no. Mum gave me some change so that I could buy myself a drink – money was so tight there was nothing spare for a social life and up until then I had no interest in going out anyway.

As I walked around the beautiful square which linked the Town Hall to our street, I could hear the songbirds starting up their exquisite evening choir and this and the freshness of the evening gave me confidence to enter the building. (There is nothing like someone trading you in for a younger version for denting that confidence!) Horribly however, as the noise and warmth of the busy gathering hit me, I realised I had probably made a terrible mistake. Just about everyone I knew in the town was there from every church in the area and they were all there in couples. It was too late now though as in the brightly lit hall I had been spotted from across the crowd by a particularly friendly and cheerful soul who called me over to her table full of people. Quickly I sat down on the only empty chair; the empty chair that was next to Daniel Barton.

I absolutely believe that when we truly give ourselves to Christ, turn away from the past, ask for His forgiveness, worship Him as Lord of all and allow Him to live in us, we enter into infinite possibilities of restoration. In fact, the hope that we have in Jesus is so sure and strong that He will use every last thing in our lives – past, present and future – to restore us. He sets us apart for Himself in order to work in our lives; He organises our circumstances if we allow it so that we grow to be more and more the person we would have been had we been born into a perfect world and had never sinned; we have the potential to become the person which He created us to be in the first place. In this process also comes the potential to restore and reclaim the world around us, the communities in which we live, to influence our society for the good, to improve people's lives and undo some of the mayhem wrought by fallen humanity (including ourselves) and the devil. This rights many wrongs and, of course, brings glory to the Lord.

Jesus was born into this fallen world, but He never sinned so He could take our place on the cross. It was my cross He carried to that hill, it was yours, and on it was nailed every wrong thought, feeling and action the world has ever seen. That is what killed Him – our sin. Through the power of His risen life, He now takes our broken and spoilt lives to make them well again, in every sense of the word. He is our peace, our 'Shalom'; healing and wellbeing in all aspects of our existence.

To do this in my life the Lord was going to have to almost start again from the beginning. This is why I now believe that He took me through the horror of having my family torn apart. Despite the trauma and pain which we all suffered I can truly thank Him because without that I would never have known the love of my life, without whose love I would not have been able to truly experience God's love for me.

To be loved unconditionally is one of the greatest gifts that a human being can receive. I know I am immensely fortunate to have met and married the person who would love me without reservations for the rest of my life on this Earth. Of course, I did believe that God loved me by now but I had no idea what that love fully meant as love had been a much mis-used word in my life because those who should have loved me and cared for me had done a poor job of representing what love is. Naturally, human love is limited but it is not the distorted or perverted emotion that I once believed it was. In action, in its truest form, even human love is wonderful. Divine love is obviously on a completely different level and it is only now that I am beginning to have a true understanding of God's love at all.

The Father's love, His Agape love, is far, far away from our understanding of human love anyway. It transcends human love as Niagara Falls transcends a garden sprinkler; it is beyond our capacity to comprehend. It is His active love through His Son for His people, totally undeserved, totally unconditional, incapable of failing. This love can only be experienced through the Lord and we are only able to express this kind of love as we remain in Him.

Apart from all of this though, even the idea that a man could be faithful and loving, could put up with me for any length of time, could accept me for myself, was an alien concept which would take some proving. When He brought Daniel into my life this was exactly what God had in mind. Through this relationship He would show me that not all love is temporary and fatally flawed; that not all men are rats who only want to use you and then discard you when it is inconvenient. More importantly, He was to open my heart and mind to the possibility that His love was exceptional and perfect. Up until this moment I really did not realise I was in fact a man hater – not a happy state to be in for anyone, but especially not someone with three little boys who were growing up fast.

Daniel was sitting casually leaning back in his chair, looking very smart in suit and tie and quite handsome. He had already consumed a couple of drinks and was super relaxed and chatty. I, on the other hand, sat stiffly in my chair and only loosened up a little when Gill poured a glass of wine for me out of her personal bottle. Not used to alcohol this did help me to unwind and I was gradually able to lift my eyes from my feet and gaze around the softly lit dance floor. It was extremely crowded, almost everyone I had met in the wider Church in our town was there and, as I had first noticed, everybody was a couple. The music was loud and the place was stifling and I just wanted to bolt for the door. Long before the days of mobile phones I had no way of checking on the children so consequently I was keen to get home to them; at least that was the excuse I made for myself.

Daniel, however, was really enjoying the evening, seeming to want to know all about me. I was a rampant Bible basher in those days and so I never let an opportunity to give someone the Good News pass me by. Sadly, I probably put more people off than I led to Christ, but Dan seemed very interested until I told him he was a sinner and needed saving. He actually thought he was a Christian and just could not accept what I was saying. He thought he was a good person who had never done anything that was terribly wrong so why would God reject him, why on earth would he need forgiving? Then when someone came round taking photographs, he put his arm around me for a pose and I told him to get off as I was a married woman. Yes, I was obviously keen to make a good first impression!

Actually, at the beginning I was not in the least bit interested in Daniel Barton romantically. For one thing I was still praying with my children every night for their daddy to come back and furthermore he was not a Christian. It had been horrendous living with a man who had gone back to living as an unbeliever; there was no way I would get involved with someone who had absolutely no clue about what it was to be saved. Daniel just was not my type (which should have been good news as 'my type' had made less than successful husbands), he was far too young and we had nothing in common. Anyway, I was still married, as I had just told him. These marriage vows had meant something to me because I had made them to the Lord.

Daniel assured me he just wanted to be a friend but over the next few months our paths crossed again and again. A mutual acquaintance had got him involved in her

Tradecraft work so when she came to my house to host a Tradecraft party he tagged along with her. She even suggested that he returned to mend my hat stand, which I really did not seem to have any say in. When this happened, the kids took to him straight away and conned him into taking them to the shop (where he probably bought them all sweets!). They arrived back with a slightly bemused Daniel (who we now knew as Dan) and he said that 'four children were quite a lot but I suppose you could get used to it'!!

I have since learnt that he often says out loud exactly what he is thinking, almost without realising it; this trait has got him into trouble at times throughout his life but was quite endearing at the time.

After this he asked me to play badminton with him so I invited a couple of young women from my church along, hoping to distract him away from any interest he might have in me. He wrote me a lovely letter offering to be my friend but that just seemed an impossibility and I was very guarded.

Now, shortly before I met Dan a strange thing had happened. Not long before Sonia and I had prayed the 'ideal husband' prayer I was reading my Bible one evening and clearly heard that still small voice of the Holy Spirit in my heart telling me to let the unbelieving partner go. How could I do this when God had told me clearly not to divorce John, even though I had grounds because he had admitted his adultery? Just after I had found out about his girlfriend, and because this had made me furious, I had started to divorce him twice but had been stopped by the Lord and had realised that I should not be the one to irrevocably break this marriage as my children would not thank me for it. I also knew I would eventually have to forgive the man and the anger that I felt would need to be given to God for me to move on.

I prayed the prayer in obedience, however, giving the relationship to the Lord; truly from my heart I began letting my errant husband go. Astonishingly, the next morning divorce papers plopped through my letterbox. He was divorcing me! After two years' separation the only condition for the divorce to go through was my consent – my 'letting the unbeliever go'. So, again in obedience to God, I did exactly that. Although I had no way of knowing this, my obedience opened up the way for Him to bring Dan into our lives. God always honours and blesses our obedience, but in this case without my obedience the rest of my life on Earth would have been totally different. The Lord could not have allowed me to meet another prospective partner.

There was still the problem that Dan was not saved because, even though neither of us realised it, each time we saw each other our affection for each other was growing; he was becoming a dear friend. I even remember sending up one of those 'arrow prayers' that we pray, where we are almost just thinking out loud to God, 'Lord please save Dan for me' I murmured. Then in mid-February I had an amazing phone call.

The evening before, there had been a Valentine's Day party at church and we had all gone along. Once more I had felt so alone and miserable as many couples, most of them with their children, were there together. My four little ones had joined in happily with their friends in the large back room where all such functions took place, playing games, eating party food and running around noisily. As I sat miserably alone the Lord spoke to me and said 'I will be your Valentine' and once more I had to accept that this may be His will for me; to be a single parent who was destined to raise the four on my own.

The next evening, I was hosting a small Bible study group at my house – we called it the chocolate Hobnob group as my friend Suzy would bring round those particular biscuits. A few of us would look at the Bible together whilst munching on bickies and drinking coffee, also provided by the group. The phone went and when I answered it Dan was on the other end telling me that the night before he had given his heart to the Lord Jesus. I knew he had been going to a friend's church regularly and reading his Bible but this announcement was a complete surprise. So faithless of me as only the week before I had asked the Lord to save him for me!

'Oh! you must come round and tell the group here,' I said, putting the phone down and looking in the hall mirror. Rushing upstairs I quickly put on a bit of makeup, although it was not until I came downstairs again that I asked my image in the mirror what on earth I was doing making an effort. Why was I trying to impress and who was I trying to fool? There must have been serious feelings there already but when the doorbell rang and I opened it to him 30 minutes later I knew. I was in love with him. It was as if someone had switched on a light and I just knew he was the love of my life.

That night after he left my house he rang me and we were on the phone for several hours. In fact, over the next few days we had many extremely long calls that gave us the chance to get to know each other and realise we had all these feelings for each other. He told me about his first wife and her adultery; I told him about my marriage to Clive and my betrayal of him. When I realised that Dan did not condemn me for this, despite the fact that his ex-wife had done the same thing, for the first time I realised that God had forgiven me. I did not have to spend the rest of my life in misery because of it. God really had forgiven me and I was brand new. It was as if in the light of Dan's conversion I could see again the greatness of God's mercy and grace towards me afresh. We spent hours on the phone telling each other our life stories and praying about the future. Amazingly the phone bill was the same as usual at the end of the quarter, long before free call packages were invented.

We prayed about the children accepting him, as Dan said we had no hope of a future together if they did not accept this new man into their lives. A few days after this prayer, out of the blue, Isaac told me he wanted Dan as a dad and Caleb (who had always said he did not want me to marry anyone else) said that if his dad was not coming back he would like Dan as a dad. Miraculous! Without this we could not have remained as friends let alone anything else.

The next two weeks sped by. I knew straight away that I should not see Dan again until after my divorce, especially alone – it was not possible for us to pretend that we did not love each other. I knew that I was so desperate to be with this man who loved me it was not going to be easy to obey God. Even though I had given consent ages before to the divorce it was still going through its process. Now that we realised we had feelings for each other we could not see each other until the Decree Absolute; that was my firm conviction. There was no way we could begin to build a family on rocky foundations – that had been part of the problem in the marriage with John.

Dan and I must build our marriage, our restored family, on Christ and Him alone and that would take obedience. We had not even kissed but there was no way we could pretend this was just a friendship and we had to separate. The problem was I just could not do it on my own. After telling Dan this I rang him the next day to tell him we would need help.

We arranged to speak to our respective church leaders. His said there was no problem but my pastor had a completely different response and I knew what was coming as we walked up to Denis and Pat's house in the early evening a few days later. Denis was a real man of God and lived and taught the Bible. If anyone was going to give us the right answers it would be him, although they may not be the answers we wanted to hear. In fact, I knew what he would say but it came as a great shock to Dan who had been a Christian for only a few weeks. Nevertheless, he knew that whatever Denis said I would abide by it.

At first Denis was suspicious as he could see that the depth of our feelings was great and unlikely to have just developed over a fortnight, but I think he believed us when we said we had had no idea that these feelings were growing before we even realised they existed. We sat in his front room, nervously awaiting his answer, but when it came we were both devastated.

'You must break off all contact with each other until after the divorce is absolute – there must be no meeting, no phone calls, no notes. Nothing.' This was far more than I was expecting, much more of a total separation than even I had imagined.

We both agreed to this straight away. I knew I had to do that as I had known really that this was God's will. Poor Dan had no choice as he had always known I would do whatever Denis had said. We walked home that night the three and a half miles from Denis's and it took a very long time for Dan to leave me at the other end. We thought it would be three months until we could see each other but in fact it took six for the divorce to finally be done. If we had known that I doubt we could have faced the future. Little Caleb woke up well after midnight as we were struggling to say goodbye (he was the one child who never woke up during the night!) and climbed onto Dan's knee. Gently Dan explained he was not going to be able to come round to see us all for a while and asked Caleb to look after me. That Saturday when their dad came to take the kids out for the day Caleb refused to go with his siblings for the first time ever; instead he stayed behind to do just that, look after his mum.

The next six months were some of the hardest I have ever known. It is true to say that the Lord takes us through some difficult experiences but I have learnt that this is only for our welfare. At the time, however, it was almost more than I could bear. Here was a man who loved me and my children, who wanted to look after me and my children and help me to bring them up. He actually wanted to share our lives and serve the Lord with me and we were not going to be able to see him, speak to him, or even contact him. Instead, we had promised to write to each other every day without sending the letters to each other. We agreed to keep these letters until we could be together so we could then share the time which we had spent apart. This saved my sanity and every night when the kids were asleep I would sit down to 'tell' Dan all about my day, sharing with him all the ups and downs of family life. All the things that I wanted to tell him – everything I had done or the kids had done and my longing to see him.

It was not too bad when the children were there but the Saturdays when they went out with their dad were awful and one particularly bad one I lay on my face before the Lord and begged Him to allow me to see the love of my life. That was the day of a friend's wedding and I went along to church to celebrate with her. During the ceremony the Lord told me that this would be me and Dan in a year's time and I floated across the road and into the local Christian bookshop for a coffee. Sitting at the bar was Dan and my heart leapt as he turned to say hello. Those precious few moments were a real lifeline that God had thrown to me and that chance meeting kept me going for weeks.

The divorce took an age to go through because I had started proceedings and then stopped them when the Lord told me not to do it. I had been warned of this by three different women of God who had reminded me of the story of Jacob and Rachel in the Bible. He had to wait twice as long as he thought he would for his bride and the six months which we had to wait for the divorce was twice the norm. Again, I asked God for sight of Dan and found that we had both booked in for the afternoon at a children's work training session at a local Anglican church. We spent the afternoon together along with several hundred other trainees, but as I left I realised that seeing me like that was killing him, so I stopped asking the Lord for any more 'chance' meetings.

In August the children and I went off to Wentworth House in the Northeast for their annual Bible week and while we were away the divorce was finally absolute. I rang Dan from the house and we spoke for the first time about our future together. When the five of us arrived back at the house in the Midlands several days later he was waiting for us with banners and balloons and all manner of treats. I had a tatty large brown envelope full of notes and scraps of paper where I had scribbled down each evening what had gone on during my long days while we were apart, whereas Dan had bought me a beautiful pink jewellery box (which I still have) that was full of long, loving letters and wonderful cards (which I also still have). Perhaps he was much more of a romantic or maybe he just had a bit more time!

We were all so glad to see each other and it was not long before we were to meet with the elders of our church to discuss our plans. Slightly nervous, we waited for them to arrive at the house but we were both amazed and delighted at their decision. They said they had decided that because of our obedience in staying apart for half a year, plus the fact that we were both the innocent partners in the divorces which we had both been through, they would marry us in church the following summer. From then on Dan spent much of his waking moments at our house and we began to build our family together. Needless to say, there were things in both our personalities which needed to adapt and we both found this process difficult at times, but we put the Lord in the centre of everything we planned and did and were on course for a wonderful life together. .. that is until I discovered, to my dismay, that he was not perfect.

We now joke about that so many years later because, of course, neither am I, but then I still think I was looking for that elusive perfect man to care for me. Paradoxically at the same time secretly I still believed that all men were rats and would ultimately let me down. So there we were with my really unrealistic goals and a doom-filled, self-fulfilling prophesy mentality yet again to potentially blight our future. Dan also had tremendous insecurities from his first marriage, added to the fact that he had always been a nervous person who lived on his nervous energy. This was going to be different though; this time God was involved from the foundations upwards and when He builds a house it stays built, adversity and trials making it stronger instead of tearing it apart.

When I discovered that Dan had a bit of a temper and could be rather unpleasant in the heat of the moment when we had a row it was devastating. His insecurities made it very hard for him when he got things wrong in our relationship and to say we had communication difficulties is a vast understatement. This also made me aware that I was still carrying some of the old insecurities and anxieties which had helped to destroy my two previous relationships. I did consider not marrying again, thinking that perhaps I was just not capable of making marriage work at all. Two pieces of advice helped with this. First, at an outreach supper the speaker talked to us afterwards and said I should seriously think about the sensible way forward for me and the children's future if I chose to stay alone. We had shared my doubts, my insecurities and Dan's unpleasant side and he was really pragmatic, helping me to put this in perspective. Could I actually cope with his temper, his imperfections which were what actually made him human, just like me? Could I accept that this man, who obviously loved me passionately, was also emotionally immature in much the same way as I was? Could I face the fact that he was an imperfect human being like me who would occasionally get things wrong but, unlike the other men in my life, always seek my good, never desert me or give up on the relationship?

Then there was Sue's advice. A dear friend, still, she simply said that, as marriage was so hard, if we could live without one another we should. That sealed it. We knew we could not live without each other and decided to trust God for the rest.

I have to say that over the last 34 years or so the Lord has worked on us both and we no longer have those terrible times – in fact we are closer and more in love with each passing year. Of course, we have both had to change to make this happen. In the process we have found the secret of a lasting and fulfilling relationship – die to self. Any relationship requires this to truly work. We need to die to the old self-life of sin and selfishness in order for Christ to live in us by His Holy Spirit. In marriage this is especially important because this relationship has the power to give great joy and blessing, but equally the power to wound and destroy like no other. The grace of God has enabled us to forgive each other, to move on through some pretty challenging issues, but His love has remained with us, and our love, both for Him and for each other, has never wavered. We look forward to eternity together – no longer as man and wife, but always and forever together with the Lord.

10. The Journey

Four children, two dogs, a scruffy black and white cat called Kipper and two adults, unprepared for life in such a busy household, we set off on our adventure together with a house full of bustle that was inevitably a bit chaotic at times.

The wedding itself was a 'Fairytale' as friends rallied round to help organise the event. To be able to share this joy with family and friends from our church was wonderful. We even had a very short honeymoon in Stratford-upon-Avon; it lasted only for the weekend because the children were left with grandparents. We made a promise to each other to go back when we had a proper length of time to spend there and we have done this over the years with knobs on – probably spending many weeks there in total!

We were very happy, always busy but adapting pretty well to our large family in a big house full to overflowing. Very soon after the honeymoon we found ourselves to be expecting a baby, which delighted the children, promising to make our not-so-little family complete. Around 12 weeks into the pregnancy I found myself giving this child to the Lord at the Sunday morning worship service as I had already dedicated the other four to Him when they were small.

God took me at my word, taking that child to Himself the next day when I suffered an early but nonetheless devastating miscarriage.

The children were amazing once again, showing such tremendous faith, re-assuring me that I would see this little one again in Heaven, but it was hard to accept this straight away. My dream of having a child with Dan was not to be and I knew quite soon after this that God did indeed know best;

Dan had always felt that he would not have children who were biologically his and he had little time to bond with this unborn child. The Lord knew, even if we did not at the time, that the addition of a small baby to our already hectic life would have been too much. We already had four children whose little world had been shattered when their dad had left home, especially as I had been a bit of a wreck for a while after this cataclysmic event. Four children who would need all the love, comfort and time we could give to them in addition to the moulding of ourselves in order to make this relationship work. It was not hard to see that the Lord knew what He was doing in denying us a baby together; it just took some time and a lot of prayer for me to accept this.

Living together in the large, rundown old vicarage that we had inherited from the old life was proving a strain financially. It was far too big for us anyway so we sold up and bought our first home together. Still a large house it took all our resources, but I even learnt to drive again, finally passing my test which enabled us to buy our first car.

Money was now a bit less tight, but Dan and I were concentrating on the children's welfare and needed little for our own times together. There was very little left after all the bills were paid but we knew God would supply all our needs (I had in fact prayed for a husband on the basis that if I needed one the Lord would provide, as He promises to supply all our needs. I had also prayed that he would be good with money because I had been in a dire financial state when I was a single parent.)

More often than not Dan and I would go for a walk when we had time alone while the kids went to their dad's and even when we did go out we thought spending a tenner was extravagant. There was always enough though as God faithfully kept His promises to us. I had even started doing some tutoring at Burton College and begun to plan recording a CD. People were always asking if I had my songs on tape – during my lonely, broken years the Lord had given me a few beautiful songs to share with the church – and Dan and I thought it was time to invest in studio time. My wonderfully talented friend Basil agreed to do the sound engineering and many musician friends from the churches in Burton collaborated to make 'My Wonderful One' a great little EP. Our artistically talented middle son, Caleb, produced the cover sleeve for this, heralding his future time at art college.

The church we were part of gave us a wonderful opportunity to set up a team ministry together, heading up a monthly outreach evening called Street Light Plus. This was an adult version of Street Light, a youth outreach which encouraged young people from our church to bring their unsaved friends to a youth event. In our case we, and our team of good friends, put together a concert and meal where, again, Christians could bring their friends into a relaxed atmosphere in which they could experience friendship and music without coming to a church service. For Dan and me it was good to be in ministry together, although sometimes the pressure of that was hard, revealing some of the issues that still needed dealing with.

We booked Christian artists and bands and provided good food and a non-alcoholic bar. People from all over the town with a wide variety of church backgrounds brought their friends to these events, encouraging us all for a while to believe this would lead to them sharing their faith. After a time though it became apparent that the Christians were coming to enjoy these evenings, which was good, but failing to bring non-Christians with them. At this point we brought the concerts to a halt, celebrating our wonderful team by cooking them a massive Chinese meal. (I am not sure how we did this, my memory has us on roller skates but I am sure that is just my imagination!)

The children were growing in the Lord and both Isaac and Caleb asked to be baptised at this time, wanting to make a public declaration of the faith which they had both come to as young boys. Isaac was ever vocal about his faith and at one time had been bold enough to speak at his Sunday school class's service on the biblical Joseph's imprisonment in Egypt. 'Aunty Elizabeth', Isaac's Sunday school teacher, had her whole class praying for persecuted and imprisoned Christians in Russia. My eldest son preached that morning with such fervour and deep, childlike faith, prophesying that if we believed even the Berlin wall would come down. Very shortly after this it did in fact fall.

God was doing wonders in us all and for the first time He gave me the confidence to really sing for His Glory. He had always opened up opportunities to sing in worship meetings and the wonderful songs which He had given to me were amazing examples of this, but now I was able to become more involved in music as I was asked to join the Youth for Christ worship team as a singer. This involved being part of a talented group of musicians who would be invited to minister at various church events in the town. We were privileged to join many other Christians who together made up the wider Church. Some of this involved street evangelism but the most exciting was the involvement in the town carnival when I was asked to perform some of my songs for the crowds.

There had been bigger venues, the Harrogate Conference centre being one, but this was the first time I would be singing in a large open-air event. The only trouble was it became a bit too much for my ego. I struggled to keep the line between worship and performance clear, constantly battling with the need to get the approval and applause of the crowd. This was probably because of my insecurity, finding it hard to accept that God loved me for me, not for what I could do. I felt that the Lord was asking me to lay down the music ministry – which I did – for a year. This was important as it also gave Him the chance to help me to deal with the pride that being in the public eye often fosters. It also gave Him the chance to help me to deal with the rejection which had followed me around all my life and which was only really pushed away when I was singing in public. This of course did not deal with it and that is what was needed. Through the love and acceptance of Dan and my friends in the church and the power of the Lord to heal I was finally delivered of that besetting evil. At last, I knew that I was loved and accepted for who I was and not for what I could do. When the music became an active part of my life again it was much more firmly in its place.

For the first time in many years finances were not an issue as my dear husband was good with money (one of the things on my list of attributes which Sonia and I had prayed over!). We had growing needs in our growing children but Dan really wanted to be the provider for his now enormous family and his profession as a draughtsman, though not fantastically well paid, made it possible for him to do this.

This was all about to change as God unfolded yet another of those mighty and wonderful trials that He alone can use to change us from the inside, to teach us to trust Him more and to grow in faith; these are often painful, sometimes lasting a long time if we are slow to embrace His providence and learn from them.

BTR was a family institution in the Barton household. Dan, his father, brother and sister had all worked there for years and he had worked nowhere else since leaving school.

Apart from a short period many years earlier, when they had made him redundant for six months then taken him back on, he had laboured away in their drawing office as an engineering draughtsman. I would not say he loved his job; it seemed stressful and tiring – so much so that he often came in from work, ate tea and fell asleep on the settee. Naturally this meant he also avoided some of the strain of family life that had been so suddenly thrust upon him.

It was a stable environment, however, and this was important as we were only just beginning to adapt to the large and complicated set of relationships a step-family generates. Our relationship was difficult at times but I would only let the cracks show when the children were at their dad's because I wanted them to feel safe, secure in their new family unit. We had only been married a year and just bought our first house together when the first real blow came. Jobs were uncertain and Dan's in particular dodgy. It was a relief after the threat of job losses loomed when it happened – like the sword of Damocles' finally falling. He was made redundant for the second time, by the same firm.

Now, to put this in context, yet again it became obvious that the Lord had a plan all along and this was how he was going to work it out, but we were still not able to see that. Neither of us had yet learnt that He was in control at all times, that nothing ever happens to His people without a reason. We did learn another great lesson during this period however: never say 'never' when the Lord is in your life. He has a way of re-organising things to go according to His plans and not our own.

Shortly after we had moved house a pastor from a church in Malawi visited our town and we had invited him for a meal. Booker Banda's work was amazing and the church he led had just opened a school in Malawi. Education is the key in many developing nations to release people from poverty. When he heard that I had been a teacher he was excited and jumped around our house laughing and praising God. 'Oh! you must come and teach in Malawi!' he cried.

'No, no', I protested, 'I am never going back into teaching,' sure that this was the end of the matter; although I was unhappy about disappointing this African man of God. He just smiled enigmatically and told me that I must never say never where the Lord is concerned. I was soon to learn this the hard way.

Within a very few weeks of Dan's redundancy it became obvious that I had little choice but to return to teaching. Having given it up to try to pursue a career in music many years before, I was pretty sure this was going to be hard. However, two things were very different this time. First of all, I had life experience, lots of it, which made me a much better candidate for the role and, more importantly, I had the Lord Jesus in my life and He was going to make a huge difference.

Teaching is a difficult profession and for me one with which I had struggled as a twentysomething who was carrying a large amount of baggage. Anxiety and depression had been my constant companions which made standing in front of a bunch of kids difficult to say the least. The strain of teaching had seen me on Valium at that time and eventually led me to work part-time. Now we were in great need of another salary as all the work Dan could get was a series of paper rounds. He could have got work as a draughtsman in another city but we had four children who needed to be kept settled in their new home and their schools. Also, their dad was once again living nearby and for this and for many reasons we could not uproot them.

So back to school I went, this time with Jesus alongside me, which was a big improvement. The classroom was not any easier – if anything behaviour had deteriorated along with society around us – but I was not alone in it anymore. As with the rest of life, having the Lord of Heaven and Earth alongside you makes a huge difference. Not too long afterwards Dan did get a full-time job with a real salary but I continued to work part-time and do supply teaching until I was offered a permanent position at a nearby special school. I became head of music and was employed for three days a week to devise a curriculum and write schemes of work and lesson plans. I loved the work and, because I wanted to do my best for the students, when the headteacher asked me to go full-time I could not resist. The salary was good and I felt valued and needed at work (which I did less and less at home as the children turned into teenagers!) Foreign holidays beckoned, new kitchens tempted; there was suddenly going to be spare money and it was captivating.

Teaching music and drama to children with special needs full-time was a challenge in itself which also added to the stress levels at home; however, the straw which eventually broke the camel's back (or in this case saw me floored by a prolapsed disc – literally) was my unwise decision to start a speech and language degree at a nearby university. I had always wanted to do a degree because I probably should have done one earlier but this was just too much for me, even in my Superwoman T-shirt, to manage. The course was interesting and I loved being at university, sometimes physically present at weekend residentials, but mostly online and remotely studying. The school had given me a day each week to study and Dan was incredibly supportive, but even so the workload was immense both at home and at work.

This had been going on for almost two terms when one early evening I bent down to get something from the fridge and fell to the floor in agony. It left me crawling out of the kitchen to ring for help, long before the days of mobile phones in every home, as Dan was at work and the kids at their dad's.

So here I pause to look at the last few paragraphs and realise that I have covered quite a few years of our new life together as a family under God. Between our wedding day and this day were about ten years of hectic, wonderful, difficult and sometimes challenging days. Bright times of seeing the children bond to Dan and dark days of my lurking fears that this too would go horribly wrong. Faithful days when we saw God heal and restore our family and faithless days when we would argue and stress over stupid, meaningless things which threatened to undermine our unity. But all the way through He was with us and that wonderful love which He had given us for each other when He brought us together was the cement which would not let us split. All the way through those first ten years of our married life Jesus was with us, restoring us as individuals and binding us together as a couple. We were truly becoming one flesh.

The Lord gave us opportunities to serve Him together both in and outside the home, and we began to trust Him for all our needs as we saw these met, sometimes miraculously (and at the last minute!). Our children, for Dan has always really thought of the four of them as his own, were becoming more settled and we were building a stable, secure and happy family home. Each summer we would take our holiday at Wentworth Bible week in Aldborough where the whole family received restoration and healing through the ministry of the Holy Spirit. So much was given back to us emotionally and we all benefited. The kids loved the youth camp and made many good friends from all over the UK. They were becoming teenagers – at one point we had four teenagers – and life could be very busy and sometimes stressful. We were growing and developing in the Lord but, as my friend Kevin says, the scaffolding was still up and, although God was rebuilding us, sometimes the old fears broke through and threatened to overwhelm me. The rejection issue may have been dealt with but fear was still very much part of my life.

One of the worst fears which haunted me throughout this first decade of marriage was that my dearest Dan would leave me, as all the important men in my life had done before. There had been my dad, who actually never came back to live with us after I was born; my first husband, Clive, who told me he was not going to live with me the day that we came back from honeymoon and, of course, John. He, who had professed a faith in Christ, fathered my wonderful children and then, unable to cope with family life and my emotional instability, left also. These incidents had left their mark, wounds which had still to be cleaned and healed. The fact that John left after I had trusted God with the relationship made it all the more difficult to trust either Dan or the Lord and I was seemingly too stubborn to let go. With the benefit of hindsight, now I see that I just could not face up to the fear and let Jesus deal with it. How many times do we think we can hide things from Him, or in fact anyone else. It is only ourselves which we fool. This head-in-the-sand act was to create unbearable tension which inevitably led to a complete physical breakdown that came like a bolt from the blue just a few weeks before Dan's 40th birthday.

I had been planning to organise a big family celebration for him, complete with custard pies to be thrown in his direction (something he had always wanted to experience).

So, there I was, crawling on my stomach into the living room, ringing for help that came in the form of my dear friend Sonia. The doctor came and went and I was dosed up on heavy-duty pain relief. Dan arrived back from work a little later and I was half-carried, half-dragged up to bed where I stayed off and on for the next ten weeks. This was the end of the road, the end of myself, the end of life as I knew it, but in God's economy it was to be a beginning.

There had to be a new beginning in a way because, despite all the years of learning to know the Lord, I really was so wrong about Him and His ways. This period of incapacity was to teach me more about these two subjects than the twenty years before it: how to trust Him, follow Him, depend on Him in a completely new way. In the book of the prophet Isaiah God's Word says

"...But those who hope in the Lord will renew their strength. They will soar on wings like eagles;" Isaiah 40 v 31

Whereas I was struggling to walk to the loo!

11. Hope Springs

When I started this book, several years ago, I asked the Lord why He wanted me to write it. He said it was to give people hope: hope of a new life in Him, hope of forgiveness and redemption; hope of a real life, a life of promise, of purpose and fulfilment; hope of a future with Him that is never ending. As I said earlier in this account, out of the sow's ear of my broken, mangled life He is making a silk purse of grace and love. From the rebirth at the moment of salvation to the promise of rebuilding our broken lives we are destined to return to the Garden, Eden, that first place of friendship and fellowship with God, which is only possible through the gift of His Son.

My broken body, unable to function properly and, according to my doctor, never likely to be anything else, was not supposed to be the outcome of this. In the end the doctor was wrong and it was not to be as he forecast.

The terrible pain of the first few days was masked by heavy doses of co-codamol, so that first period is a real blur. The medics told me to lie flat on my back because the leaked spinal fluid from the prolapsed disc had caused damage in the surrounding area. I was not going to argue with them as any attempt at movement was excruciating despite the pain killers. In the couple of years prior to this event my lower back had been quite weak, resulting in two much more minor episodes which needed only a few days of lying flat to restore full mobility. This time, however, the disc was truly slipped and I was in a mess. At the special school where both Dan and I were now working, we were sometimes forced to restrain the students for their own protection. This had put a huge strain on my back and after the first two events where my back had been in distress the doctor had advised me not to do the restraints. This was not possible in the working situation at this particular school and inevitably the final injury came.

For days the only way I could reach the loo was by using a walking frame, which gave me very slow and limited mobility, even with the high doses of painkillers that were a constant part of my life. Eventually the medics sent an ambulance for my transport to the hospital for X-rays; these showed a curvature to the spine, two worn vertebrae and very little signs of hope for a recovery. My doctor gently broke the news to us both soon afterwards that this was pretty much going to be my life from now on – I would be disabled. What he did not know of course that bleak March morning was that God had called us to mission in Albania, which was going to be difficult to fulfil if my physical state did not improve drastically. One cataclysmic event had not spoilt God's plans for me and my husband, and this also would not do that. Dan and I looked at each other straight after the doctor's prognosis. We did not need to say anything; we both knew what our response would be. 'We're Christians and we're going for a miracle,' I said to my GP. I am not sure what he thought, but the doctor's response was tactful: 'Come back and see me when you get one,' he replied gently, although his facial expression said something a little less convincing.

Many years earlier, when I was a baby Christian believing that my husband at the time was the Lord's, God spoke to me clearly, telling me that my husband and I would take the Gospel to the nations. When he walked out on us all I was naturally sure this could never happen, that God's plan had been thwarted by man's disobedience – either that or I had mis-heard Him, which was more likely. Then not long after Dan and I got married this prophesy was repeated at a Christian event. God had said 'my husband' and I, not John and I, would serve Him together in the nations. God is much bigger than our mistakes or men's decisions.

Dan and I were sure that Albania was the country we were to go to but we knew nothing about it. We had booked our first family holiday in Greece two summers before my back went, on the tiny Island of Corfu, and were amazed to find that the Albanian coast was just across a narrow strip of sea from there. We took the kids on a tour of the island, the tour bus stopping in Kassiopi, a beautiful village in the north of Corfu, and found ourselves gazing across at Saranda, Albania. We did not realise that the city of Saranda was to become such an important part of our lives. Then, a year after this, we had taken another trip to Corfu so that we could have our first visit on the organised day trip while friends stayed behind with the kids in Corfu. The summer to come we were already planning a longer stay in Saranda so we could get a better feel for the place.

The flights were already booked for our return to Corfu so that we could combine a week-long visit to Albania with a holiday in the summer of that year. The beleaguered country had just opened up again after the pyramid-selling scandal had thrown it into terrible turmoil and anarchy for six months, so we were determined to take another trip over the narrow channel that separated the two very different countries.

Now, it seemed, the visit would be impossible – in fact most of life would be extremely difficult with my future very uncertain; according to the doctor I would probably never work again and simple household jobs would be a challenge. As I lay there on my back, for the first time in a long time God had got my full attention. I realised I had been running, in much the same way as Jonah had been when he set off in the opposite direction to Nineveh. Jonah had ended up in the belly of a whale, trapped and unable to escape by his own efforts. This was very similar; I was trapped in a body which would not function properly and there was nothing I could do about it.

I had been running from the truth about my fears concerning Dan and other women, concerning the future of our life together. Consequently, I had been running from the Lord and myself because of my refusal to face the truth. I was helpless and alone for much of the time as Dan was at work, the kids were at school and the bedroom became my world. A tiny portable TV became my window on the rest of the world but the Lord became my close companion during this time, speaking into my heart so clearly and, for the first time in years, I was listening. This was of course because, for the first time in years, I was still enough to listen. Due to my 'running' I had kept myself so busy with work, the house, a degree course, singing (and any other activity that made sure I was fairly exhausted most of the time) that He did not get a look in.

What I heard was not always easy to hear – His love for me was clear, His comfort palpable, His care through my wonderful family amazing, but He helped me to see that it was not Dan that I did not trust, but Him. I had not trusted Him with the marriage because when I had finally done that with my marriage to John He had taken him away, never to return. Now, years later, it was obvious that this had been for my own good – the relationship was toxic for us both, my life with him suffocating, but I was too afraid to realise that. The fact was that the Lord had been so good to me, He was so obviously a good, good Father who cared well for His children. This meant that my lack of trust was completely unreasonable, even insulting. How could I not trust such a wonderful God?

Sadly, I had been trapped in this by my stubborn refusal or inability to face the truth. You can push things under the carpet for a while but eventually they will trip you up, sometimes causing a nasty fall which hurts badly. This one hurt physically but also emotionally as it was impossible to be with my children during their times of need as I lay immobile and helpless. They had always been my first priority, although that might not have been obvious to them, but now there was nothing I could do to care for them – not even clearing up after them and their friends in our kitchen (which usually resembled a youth club!). They had been left too much to their own resources but Dan had to continue to go to work whilst I was trapped in my room for weeks. His average working week was 50 hours and he often had to walk the several miles home.

The load on him was immense and this was one of the most desperate reasons I had for wanting to get better – so much so that I asked the elders of the church to come round and anoint me with oil so we could pray for my healing. I knew this would be humbling for me but I needed to ask, if only out of desperation, as I watched my dear husband get more and more exhausted trying to look after me and the kids on his own. There was really no-one else around who could help us, although if he had asked his family I am sure they would have tried. However, he struggled on until it became obvious that I was going to have to humble myself by admitting to the church leaders that I had been so faithless.

Denis, who was our pastor and who had married us, was really the leader of leaders at the time so he and another of the leaders came round. Ed was fairly new to the role of elder so he came along to learn as much as to minister, I think. I was extremely low by this time; depression had always been a pit that I could fall into so easily throughout my life. Up until then I still felt as if my life was inside a long, dark tunnel, although since the Lord had begun His healing work in me I could at last see the light at the end of this tunnel. Christians who struggle with mental health issues still find it hard to talk about this, but back then no-one in the church even broached the subject..

This time I was determined to be honest with them, there was no point in them being there otherwise. I told them I had never trusted God with my marriage and that this had led to terrible insecurity, jealousy and turmoil. It spoilt our friendships with other women, especially in the Body of Christ; it led to misplaced anxiety in me and often bewilderment in Dan. Ultimately it was threatening to ruin our relationship, which had made me hide behind work or family rather than allow my husband to get too close.

The two men anointed me with oil as they prayed which helped me to repent fully for the lack of trust; to ask the Lord to forgive me and cleanse me of this and help me to surrender the marriage to Him, trusting Him completely whether Dan stayed with me or not. For the first time I realised that God was with me in this – even if Dan did do the same thing that John had done, leaving me for another woman – but more crucially I realised that if he did do that, he was not the man of God I thought he was; so, would I want him anyway? It was a win-win situation which I had not been able to see while I was blinded by fear. Fear will do that every time, trapping us in the enemy's lies, stopping us from fully appreciating or enjoying the wonderful gifts our amazing God has showered on us. Satan truly is the father of lies. Repentance however brings freedom from him as we come to the Lord fully trusting in His ways.

It was at this moment that the healing spiritually, emotionally and mentally took place. From that day I was free from that terrible fear. Physical healing took a little longer. Several weeks longer in fact.

The hospital trips by ambulance continued as physiotherapy began. Over the next few weeks there were many long, slow visits to the department's gym where I would painstakingly learn to walk properly again with only a crutch for support. These visits were indeed painful, but slowly my mobility improved, making little trips to the bottom of our little garden possible. The pain was still there but subsiding a little, making the amount of pain relief needed lessen. It looked as if the rehabilitation had begun with the prospect of being able to go out in the car coming soon. Driving had been out of the question for this whole time but it was seemingly looking hopeful that a trip with someone else in the driving seat might be on the horizon. I even walked to the corner shop one day but, whether this was a step too far or whether the disc was just too unstable, shortly after this the whole thing spun out of control – or so I thought – when, late one night, turning over in bed this time, my back went again and I was back to square one! The intense, unbearable pain came crashing back into my very being; no amount of pain relief properly deals with this type of pain apart from morphine which, naturally speaking, was my only recourse now.

Hope that the doctor had been wrong with his doom-laden prognosis had been growing as the ability to walk grew, but with this latest catastrophe my only sensation was complete despair. In my despair I literally cried out to the Lord – not for the first time in my walk with Him – this time knowing that He was my only Hope. Then the most remarkable thing happened. One of the few visibly supernatural, undeniable happenings in my life on this planet broke into my experience. I had a vision.

I saw God's hand. I knew it was God's hand just as certainly as I had known that it was God who came to me all those years before in the car. His hand, coming down from Heaven, reached into my bedroom. Where would He touch? Somewhere far more important than me I was sure; but no, this hand of God came right to me, into my back, touching the central area of pain, weakness and disability. Then He spoke into my heart very clearly, telling me that if Miguel Escobar prayed for me for healing then the Lord would heal me.

Miguel was a Chilean evangelist who had come to our home town to preach to as many Christians from different fellowships who would come to the week-long mission, which began the next day. This was clearly a great opportunity for faith to be built in His Church so there was no doubt in my mind that the Lord would do it. Dan was aware that my back had gone again so he too was ready to believe that this was God's will. He and my friend Sonia put a sunbed in the back of her car and, with me dosed up on the maximum pain relief possible, we set off for the Anglican church in a nearby suburb the next evening.

Like the disciples in the Bible account of the friends who lowered their disabled friend through a roof to get to Jesus, they half-carried me into the building, setting up the bed at one side near the back as I was very embarrassed. I thought that, hopefully, no-one would notice me there.

If only! As the building filled up it became a little more possible for my prone figure to be obscured but people still noticed that I was lying flat on my back on a sunbed in the corner – even Miguel when he arrived came over to ask why. When Dan explained what had been happening the first response from this man of God was that this night I would be healed in the name of Jesus.

Now, this woman of God was not so faith filled! Oh, after the vision earlier I knew God was going to heal me. I even knew that it would be through Miguel, but I was sure it would take the rest of the week for the faith to build in the people of God for any unbelief in any of us to be dispelled. I could not have been more wrong; how little I still understood the things of God.

There must have been a time of worship – I cannot remember – but I do remember that the co-codamol were wearing off because the pain was becoming worse. Part-way into the preach I began to think that more pain relief was needed when Miguel Escobar stopped, suddenly, mid-sentence and walked over to where I was lying (I was trying to pretend I wasn't there). As he approached my side he called out,

'In the name of Jesus – be healed!'

He told me to stand up, which I did, then to sit down, which I also did.

'How do you feel?' he asked.

'All the pain has gone,' I replied, stunned but certain that there was now no pain at all in my body.

'Walk across the front of the hall,' he said.

I began to do this but halfway across the reality of what had just happened hit me and I began to jump up and down in sheer joy at the mighty hand of the Father who had set me free from the disability. God was real, my Jesus was alive. He had broken through into this Earth once again, touching the life of His servant.

It was not just me who witnessed this though. There must have been two or three hundred people in the hall that night who saw a healing miracle in front of their eyes; hundreds of people, many of whom knew me personally or through the music ministry I had previously in the town. Christians or non-Christians they could see something wonderful had happened to me. Then, as I described it at the time, all Heaven broke loose as people came out to be prayed for or just stood with arms raised in worship, tears streaming down their faces. God was with us at Emmanuel church that night.

For the next hour or more Miguel, alongside the many church leaders who were present that night, prayed for those who came forward in faith. Many were healed or greatly encouraged; many were commissioned by God for work in many different ways. My darling husband fell down under the power of the Holy Spirit and Miguel spoke over my life an international healing ministry. Was God going to use my hands to bring His restoration to the sick in other lands? It hardly seemed possible even on that amazing night, but as I write this I am reminded of another wonderful moment that had happened many years before this in my own front room in Harrogate.

Isaac, my first-born, had always been extremely forward for his age, amazing those around him with his incredibly early grasp of language. I remember travelling across the Pennines by train to visit Mum over in Lancashire when he was only eighteen months old. People were staring at us in surprise as we chatted away in our excitement at this, his first, trip on a train. Isaac loved the Thomas the Tank Engine stories which I read to him constantly, so trains – even the non-steam engine type – were fascinating for him. The other passengers, however, must have been incredulous as a constant stream of narrative came forth from what was barely a child out of toddler stage. Not baby talk but real, intelligible conversation almost equal to that of an adult. In later years his junior school head would call us in to ask if he could attend senior school early as his IQ levels were through the roof; he would win an assisted place to private school then a scholarship to public school; Oxford University followed with a first-class honours degree to top it off, but just then he was my first baby and I had no idea how gifted he was.

His father had had eczema as a child and I had asthma so the medical profession advised us not to have this beautiful little boy vaccinated against whooping cough as there was evidence that there could be side-effects. I do not know what these side-effects might have been but nothing prepared us for the illness itself when it struck him down a little before his twenty-first month. Not just Isaac, but John and I too came down with this horrible illness. I was pregnant with our second child at the time.

The 'whoop' in the name of this hideous disease comes from the strangulated gasp at the end of each of these coughing sessions as the lungs desperately draw in life-restoring breath, seemingly just in the nick of time – bad enough for an adult, but for my little boy desperately frightening and debilitating. He reverted to a baby in a painfully short time with no speech, little movement, eating no food only bottles of milk which often came out faster than they went in if a coughing fit hit him at the wrong moment.

Antibiotic after antibiotic was prescribed to stave off infection while we watched him get weaker and weaker. The doctor visited often – comforting but chilling at the same time – until eventually Isaac began to improve gradually. What we did not know at the time was that this affliction had badly scarred his lungs so that when he eventually was up and about again he was still hampered by acute asthma.

It is strange, is it not, how remembering one thing from the past can trigger another; how the sight, sound or maybe smell of something once experienced can trigger other memories; how in later life remembering what you went in the other room for may allude you but no matter how time passes you never forget your children. They are in your heart, on your mind, even on your lips every day. Just a few moments ago I was trying to call this same Isaac on Facebook messenger, without success I may add (which was not surprising when I noticed that he had last been active on Facebook seven hours earlier, which would have been two in the morning in Chicago where he now lives with his American wife). My little boy only a very short time ago, it seems to me now, in his early forties living on another continent, far from me physically but always in my heart. My first-born, who had so nearly been lost altogether, left permanently scarred by the hideous disease which could so easily have been avoided. The awful sound of the whoop as the sufferer desperately tries to catch a breath between coughing fits, which gives it its name. However, even when He walked on the Earth Jesus sometimes allowed similar situations to develop, deteriorating on occasions beyond natural solutions, for the sake of showing His disciples who He really was. The story of Lazarus comes to mind.

For several months after the whooping cough had left our house Isaac began to regain the developmental stages which the illness had robbed him of. However, he could not exert himself in play or run around without collapsing in a coughing fit, struggling to breathe. Amazingly this was still the early years of asthma inhalers, medication only just beyond experimental stages. The device was in fact called a 'spin haler', the tiny particles used to expand the airways whirling round the inside before being breathed in. It was difficult for a small child to use, he was only two, but he did master it and it transformed our lives. With it he was almost back to normal – without it he was disabled.

Our lovely new baby boy Caleb was born, and unlike his ever-demanding sibling, he was a peaceful, placid child who slept and gurgled and was a sheer delight. Our little family was content; we were united in our care for the two boys; the church was growing fast and for a time at least we were all well. Then John went down with a terrible chest infection – again the weakness caused by the whooping cough had left us all vulnerable to these. No amount of rest or medication seemed to help so we had asked Barry, who was our pastor at the time, to come round to pray for him. I stayed downstairs with the boys while Barry went to pray up in our bedroom where the sick one had retreated several days earlier.

I cannot remember very much about that day, except that while they were praying upstairs, I had another of those extraordinary moments when the natural world we live in seems to be invaded by the life beyond time and space where we are 'seated in Heavenly places with Christ' as Paul's letter to the Ephesians tells us.

God spoke to me so clearly, not an audible voice but nonetheless unmistakeably the word of God.

'Tell Isaac to come here,' He said. 'I am going to heal him.'

Now you do not tell a very young child, however bright and articulate they are, to do this unless you are sure that this is, firstly, God speaking and, secondly, that He will do it. I had no doubt that this was the Lord speaking so, simply to be obedient, I called Isaac over and told him what I had been told by God.

'Darling, God is going to heal your asthma,' I said, instinctively putting my hands on his head. As I reached out to touch my little boy the power of God flowed down my arms and through my hands into his small frame. I knew it was the power of God, I just knew. Just like I had that night in the car, just as I had known the Easter story was true that first time I had read it after I was born again. It is God's revelation of His truth which is unmistakeable. I also knew in that instant that Isaac was healed because God does not lie.

When Barry came downstairs I told him what had happened, then later told Isaac's dad, who believed me. We decided to take our child off the medication, but keep it in the cupboard. I am not sure if this was lack of faith or pragmatism but it stayed there for many months. We never used it again. We did not need to because Isaac did not have asthma any longer. He ran and played all day long, fetching toys for his baby brother, who adored him. He was totally healed – miraculously healed – with no relapse at any time in his life.

This morning I was going through the times in my walk with the Lord when He has touched me or mine in healing and it is far more than the twice I have mentioned above – many times the supernatural has broken into the natural world in which I live at the moment – but so often I have forgotten these in the hurly burly of day-to-day life. There was, for example, the time Caleb had damaged his arm, which needed to be supported in a sling while it recovered. As he lay on the balcony of our huge house listening to worship music he was healed. He came running up to me to tell me this and then ran off to play with his siblings as if this was the most normal thing that could happen.

It is no wonder that we are told, as Jesus' disciples, not to get bogged down in the paraphernalia of the material world. He will provide all we need so we should not be worrying about things which are, after all, mostly out of our control. He is in control of our destiny ultimately; He will only allow what is for our good and for His Glory; our job is to believe this and to trust Him. Resting in the knowledge that God is good, He is all powerful and He loves us more than we can imagine. We humans find this difficult.

For me the miracle of Isaac's asthma, or lack of it, and the miracle of my new-found mobility was particularly significant. So much so the latter one was the subject of a local newspaper front page spread headlined 'A miracle for Anna!' I still do not know where the paper got the information from but a reporter arrived on my doorstep a few days later to scoop the story. There was even a television crew from *Tonight with Trevor Macdonald* who wanted to follow the story of Miguel's visit with the accompanying signs of God's presence with us.

That night though I was more concerned with consolidating the fact that I was healed, to which end I just knew that Dan and I should walk home – a three-mile journey. I was convinced that my ever-sensible husband would tell me not to be silly when I told him this, but far from trying to dissuade me he readily agreed. This was confirmation that I was correct. We got as far as town but the muscles in my legs had started to complain loudly at the walk so far causing him to suggest that we got a taxi. Significantly he then discovered he had not brought his wallet, which was very unusual for him, so we continued to walk until we made the seemingly endless journey. A dear friend from church had seen us setting off on this walk and followed in her car, convinced we would need a lift. Despite leaving straight away and following the only route home she could not find us.

When we walked into the house I asked Jacob, the only one of the children who was there, what he thought had happened. 'God's healed your back,' he said in his matter-of-fact way, as if miracles happened every day. Then he returned to his computer screen as if nothing had changed.

Everything had changed that day as we embarked on the journey of faith that was to take us thousands of miles and span years of our lives; the journey to what was to become our second home, Shiperia – the Land of the Eagles.

12. Where did twenty years go?

It is amazing to me that it was more than twenty years ago that we began our life in Albania – twenty years which also saw our wonderful four children grow up, move away, get married and have children of their own (Isaac is not a parent but a very doting Uncle!). Two decades have gone by in an instant and yet seem to have begun a lifetime ago. So much has happened, but crucially it is the people who have come into our lives to enrich them that have made the biggest impression.

It is our relationship with people that helps to make us the people we are and which are some of the greatest gifts that God can give us. One of the biggest lessons we learnt in Albania was just how much people matter and how very important friends and family are. In the late '90s this was the richness and wonder of Albanian culture which first impacted us and kept on drawing us back there; the drive for money and status in Western Europe had made these fundamental treasures seem less than their true worth as we had pursued the gods of materialism and consumerism. Even as Christians who should have known better, many of us had at times lost sight of the basic truth that the only things that will last, that are of any real value, are those things that we invest into for Eternity. Earthly treasures and the world's acclaim will all fade away; this is why we are urged throughout the teaching of our Lord to invest in things above, not things below. To give our time, talents and resources to the Kingdom of God and not of man. Love, relationships, community, family, friendship and most of all our relationship with Almighty God will outlast time and space; so little else will!

The summer when we had returned to Corfu, this time with just Jacob and his friend and our friends Rena and Phyl, we had no idea how life-changing our first brief trip over to Saranda would be. We had no idea that the city of Saranda where we first landed would indeed become our second home over the next twenty years and that we would even consider buying a holiday apartment over there many years later! But I am rushing forward and there are so many events and people and lessons we have learnt through this amazing adventure on which the Lord took us.

In our busy Western lives, so full of activity and bustle, it is so easy to forget how precious people are, how simple life needs to be and how the truth is we are meant to live in community with others. Even in the Church in the West we have become so task-orientated that the beauty of simple things often eludes us. In Albania we were to learn so much, so much more than we had ever expected.

Before we began our time over in the Med, God had been preparing us in many ways – from the missionary training which our home church had sent us on to making provision for our children, who were now growing up fast and moving away (all except for Jacob that is).

We had moved Mum down from Lancashire so that she and Roxanne could look after each other while we were away for our increasingly longer stays. The two older boys were well settled with partners and plans of their own, but Jacob was too young to stay behind alone and unwilling to come with us. We had made good friends with a lovely Greek family in Corfu who wanted him to stay with them and work in their tourist business. He loved it in the small, unspoilt, tourist village of Kassiopi and was good friends with their son, but he just did not want to leave the UK. In recent years he has told us he now knows that he should have taken that opportunity to live in Greece for a while. Hindsight is a great thing!

So, we delayed our plans and prayed. By this time we had led several missions over in Saranda and spent a month there to test the waters. We knew this was where God wanted us to be but our first priority was seeing Jacob settled and safe.

Eventually he made plans to move in with a family in a nearby town and get a job. College was going nowhere and he needed more independence. It was quite obvious to Dan and me that he did not want the restrictions that living at home inevitably brought. Unlike with his siblings, university was not an option; Jacob disliked school and found academic work far too stressful because of his unhappy relationship with written matter. His skills lay in dealing with people and were to eventually make him an excellent and successful salesman.

We had visited this family as we were a bit dubious at first but were very much reassured after having met them. He was, after all, eighteen and therefore an adult but he was still my baby and even though his siblings had all gone away from home at a similar age for university my maternal instincts made letting go just as hard each time any of them flew the nest. It took a while for him to settle, with one wobble as he came back home for a few months, but eventually he realised he needed the freedom we would not allow him; our house rules just did not suit him at all. He returned to his new home and this gave us the green light to make plans for a longer stay in Albania.

Initially we were planning to stay a year and to fund the time there by renting out our house. This was our plan but, as in so many other circumstances, God had other plans and

He was to show us His Glory by reorganising us so many times that we finally realised He is in control and we better live by the verse in Psalm 46 that tells us to 'Be still (let go and relax!) and know that I am God'. One of our first lessons as missionaries was to begin to understand that God is sovereign over all.

Land of the Eagles was, and remains, one of the most beautiful countries in the world. From the dazzling azure seas of the Adriatic to the majestic mountains of the north it presents the explorer with endless opportunities to gasp in wonder at the Creator's skills.

In the first instance though we were very unimpressed with the city we initially visited in the late 1990s. Yes, it was the city in the dream which I had when God first began to speak to us about our destiny. In this dream a bridge stretched all the way from the UK to Albania, which at that time we had only seen on a map in one of the kids' old school atlases. We walked over this bridge all the way to our destiny in the dream (if only!) and entered a beautiful place full of children laughing and dancing, colours everywhere, and happy, friendly people walking and talking all through the streets. The buildings were all elegant, nothing out of place; it was as if even the air had been coloured with bright, shiny, colourful glitter. I just knew I was very familiar with the place, as if I had visited dozens of times and was absolutely at home there.

In reality the city of Saranda we arrived at on that day towards the end of the last millennium could not have been more different.

We had purchased a day-trip pass from the local tourist office in Kassiopi, Corfu. It was expensive for a day out but we were visiting another country, the country that God had indicated was our eventual mission field and we were determined to use this opportunity to put our feet on the land itself at last. It took about two and a half hours in those days, by coach and ferry, to reach Saranda and they were still charging tourists a ridiculously large sum to gain an entry visa. Still, we knew it would be worth it to finally see the country that had been on our hearts for several years by then.

Albania in the 1990s was an unknown and largely unexplored region of Europe; it still is a bit of a mystery. Only yesterday, several decades later, I was talking to someone who expressed again the little that was known about this country in the heart of the continent of Europe. It might as well have been in Outer Mongolia as it had been separated from the rest of the world by its hardline Communist dictator for almost fifty years. Hardly anyone in England knew anything about it and we knew few people who had visited; they told tales of poverty and poor development which we were later to discover were not exaggerated.

As we crossed the narrow channel that flows, sometimes tempestuously, between Corfu and Albania we were less than impressed with the transport. The Caliopi was little more than a fishing boat which held around thirty passengers, at a push, and one car – just. Its engine strained to drag it over the choppy sea, especially as we came into open water near the middle of the ninety-minute journey. None of the crew spoke English so we were grateful for the presence of our tour guide who oversaw the safety of our passports and dealt with the entry visas. The day was bright and clear and we could see the sprawling city of Saranda quite clearly for almost half an hour before we reached shore. The view got clearer and clearer the nearer we got to land and for the last few metres we were joined by valiant young boys who swam out to meet us. It turned out that they were beggars hoping for rich pickings from these affluent foreigners.

Docking was tricky. Moorings were ancient and landfall crowded, but the greatest impression on me was that this was all very familiar. We disembarked quickly and were herded onto the tour bus that was to take us to the historic city of Butrint about half an hour away. But my first impression was confirmed as we drove through the city: I had seen it all before, I had been here before. This was the city in my dream.

Saranda was indeed the city I had seen whilst dreaming. However, it was a completely different place in reality. Everything was boarded up or smashed. No-one was in the streets. All the olive trees had been snapped off or destroyed and virtually every window on any ground floor had thick, heavy, metal bars. Every way we turned there was evidence of destruction clearly indicating that this city had been the victim of a force of violence which I had never before witnessed; as a result of this perhaps, the atmosphere was heavy, dark and full of foreboding.

Whatever had happened here? Had it once been that vibrant, happy place full of laughter and children dancing, or was I seeing into its future? One thing was for sure, something cataclysmic had gone on in this neighbourhood which demanded an explanation.

We were whisked away from all this devastation into the surrounding countryside, which was beautiful, with majestic mountains ahead of us and streams of clear water alongside. There were still signs of the madness that had gone before us as every olive grove bore signs of the destruction we had seen earlier, as someone or something had snapped off every single olive tree near to its base and every so often, by the roadside, there was a concrete bunker ominously guarding the way forward. If the olive tree is the symbol of peace this was clearly symbolic of war.

Our local tour guide was an extremely pleasant, articulate woman whose English was exceptional; Lida was in fact an English graduate who had been a teacher but now worked in the emerging tourist industry. Tourism was a fairly new phenomenon in late twentieth century Albania, although it had begun to blossom in the early part of the decade before the pyramid investment scandal near the mid-nineties rocked the nation; the scandal toppled the government and led to six months of anarchy.

Before this, during Communist times, Albania had been completely cut off from the rest of Europe; for much of the Communist era it had isolated itself from the rest of the world. For forty years the people had little or no experience or knowledge of the rest of the world or even Europe; the dictator of this totalitarian land had made sure of that.

English was a sought-after language in Albania (it still is) but then one of the main attractions was the lottery prize – a green card which would allow you to live and work in America, a dream many Albanians shared. Lida was much sought after therefore to translate and this job as a guide for our trip to Butrint (a world heritage site of extreme beauty and archaeological interest) was a plum position, paying far better than her previous post. Teachers then in Albania were paid less than waitresses. In fact, all professionals were poorly paid, a throwback to Communism's hatred of the intellectual classes; in any totalitarian regime anyone who thought for themselves (or encouraged others to do so) was a threat to be enthusiastically supressed.

We marvelled at the sights surrounding us on this trip. Roads were appalling, the coach antiquated, but the views were astonishing. Mountains stretched out on all sides, rivers ran alongside us for miles, unspoilt terrain in all directions and no buildings (apart from the concrete bunkers which littered the roadside). Lida was very attentive and fascinated to learn of our reason for being in her beloved country. When we told her that God had told us to come here and eventually move out to bring the good news of Jesus she whooped in delight and raised her arms in praise.

Lida was our first real contact in Albania and amazingly it became clear from this first meeting that she was a Christian. Her reaction was incredible because we were still looking to the Lord to confirm our calling; leaving behind our home, our jobs, and, hardest of all, our children meant we had to be sure this was what He was saying. After her initial enthusiasm she continued to explain that their church had been praying for a long time for people to come over to help with the work of the Kingdom of God as most of the missionaries had left during the anarchy. Some were forcibly removed by their own governments for their own safety but most just to protect themselves and their families from the mayhem that ensued. Our arrival seemed to answer that prayer and she wasted no time in arranging a trip to the 'English hospital' back in town once we had completed the touristy bit.

A Mercedes arrived at the restaurant where we had eaten lunch, driven by a pleasant enough chap with a large gaucho moustache and no English. He was to drop us off in the centre of Saranda next to the hospital where arrangements had been made to show us around. We were then to wait outside at the same spot for Lida and our coach to pick us up, returning us to the port and our ferry 'Home' to Corfu.

The 'English hospital', a wonderful imposing building completely intact and totally out of character architecturally, had been planned and funded by a medical charity in the UK during the early part of the 1990s. This was when the newly-elected democratic government had very little in the way of resources to run any kind of health service. It was staffed by volunteer medics, therapists and carers from the UK who came over for weeks or months at a time to donate their expertise and their time. However, at the moment it was empty of personnel as all foreigners had left during the previous year's anarchy. It had been just too dangerous to stay. The only reason that the building, along with all the medical equipment, was still completely intact was the fact that the Mafia had set armed guards around it, as marauding gangs had swept through the country destroying everything in their path. This was a bit comforting as our driver had resembled our idea of what a mafiosi driver would look like and we had been told that only the Mafia had cars during the year of anarchy.

We were shown around the facility that had become a centre to treat children with additional needs, both physical and mental, shortly before the madness had hit. Immediately upon our description of our work at Beaufort House school the administrator asked if we would consider going to work there, once we had moved over to Saranda. We replied that this was a long way off and we were not at all sure what God had planned for us to do. We left, amazed by the place and captivated by the opportunities to serve the community around us. As we waited by the entrance for our transport we began to dream of our future there.

A few minutes later, sure enough, a coach pulled up across the road and we were about to get on it when I realised this 'coach' was in fact a local bus destined for Tirane – the capital many miles to the north, and not the port half a mile away. Thankfully we let it drive away as our party pulled up to take us to the ferry.

This first visit stayed with us for many weeks as we planned our next trip which would be for longer and involve travelling in the same direction as the local bus had been going; we did indeed end up in Tirane but not until after my disabling back injury and God's miraculous intervention.

We maintained contact with Lida throughout the next year and when our feet touched land again the following summer she was there to meet us at the port and guide us through this first stay. It was Lida who had arranged for us to stay in her parents' apartment and who introduced us to her colleagues at the Lydia Foundation. This Dutch relief organisation had been bringing aid to Albania from the beginning of the opening up of the country.

There was tremendous poverty in the whole country, Saranda included, throughout the '90s and the early part of the new century. Partly through mismanagement, partly through corruption in local and central government, the people struggled on the whole to survive. Typical of many post-Communist countries, the infrastructure was incomplete or poorly maintained, which made development difficult. Just one example, which we discovered much later, was the corruption within the education system. A wealthy family – and there were a few – could buy qualifications for their offspring up to and including degree level. Even the less well-off would make sacrifices to allow their children to benefit from private tuition. Many students told us that school was where they went to meet their friends and have fun, private 'courses' were where they learnt. Sadly, they were also where you could obtain your pass marks for any exam from a few unscrupulous teachers who were desperate to top-up their meagre income. Until Albania opened up, this worked quite well unless, of course, your doctor or civil engineer had qualified by these routes.

During the dictatorship of Enver Hoxha (pronounced Hodga) Albania had been a closed country. His hardline Communism was so extreme that after falling out with the Russians he then went on to become estranged from the Chinese as their regime was not strict enough for him. During the Cold War Russia's leader, Khrushchev, had planned to put nuclear submarines into Lake Butrint, a half-hour drive from Saranda and about the same distance from mainland Greece. In exchange for this Russia offered free grain for the Albanian people in perpetuity. Hoxha would not agree, thankfully, and as this could easily have resulted in a situation similar to the Cuba missile crisis of the early sixties – but this time in the heart of Europe – we should be very grateful.

On our return to Saranda the following year we knew so much more about Albania and its chequered history; it had been important for us to begin to understand the land and its people before coming again. We had even started to learn the language. However, it was only by getting to know the culture that we were going to be able to serve the people the Lord was going to bring into our lives.

I am not sure either of us had the slightest idea how difficult it was going to be to up-sticks and move to another country, but God did and that is why I think He gave us several opportunities over the next few years before our move to live there in 2002. Even so I have to say that nothing prepared me for missing my children, although they were leaving home anyway and the move of each one to university or workplace lodgings prior to this had been horrible. Nothing prepares you for the ache in your heart as a mother when your babies fly the nest, even after their teenage years when you might have considered moving out yourself! But leaving them, the rest of our family, home, job and the safety and security of a first-world country for a less than secure future in one of the least known and poorest countries in Europe was only possible because we were going with God.

He had given us salvation, a new start, forgiveness, grace, a relationship with Him through Christ, and each other to share it with. How could we not obey His call? But it was not going to be easy.

I remember earlier on in my Christian walk realising that if I had wanted an easy life I had joined the wrong army, because an army is exactly what we join once we become members of the body of Christ. We are in a war for people's souls and although we are now on the winning side there are battles to be fought and there will be casualties. To my shame I know that there have been times when I have wanted to settle into a comfort zone and take a complacency break, especially when the weariness of trying to fight in my own strength has overwhelmed me, but once the Lord has drawn me back to Himself and restored me, the battle is the only place to be. I used to think that when I had climbed one particular mountain of difficulties and trials it would be all smooth terrain ever after but (after a short oasis of calm and rest) the next mountain appears. Usually this one is even bigger and more difficult but with each passing peak I have seemingly grown stronger faith muscles and occasionally wings. Any believer who doubts the truth of this need only read First Peter to see God's perspective!

Over the next few years things moved quite quickly. We moved Mum down to our home town so she and Roxanne could look after each other while we were living in Albania. At my wonderful daughter's suggestion we moved into a smaller, mortgage-free property, so that we could live on the proceeds of renting it out once we had gone, and we began to take longer and longer trips over the water to 'test the calling'.

Our fellowship had sent us on several training courses for missionaries and we were learning to trust God more and more for our finances, opening a 'mission bank account' for the considerable costs involved. We began to establish links with the local churches in Saranda and were privileged to head up a team from the UK and Canada to lead worship in a gospel concert which would bring all the churches in the city together for the first time. The real crunch came when we spent our first extended stay of a month – a stay which almost made us give up the whole idea altogether. I think we had underestimated the opposition.

Our first longer stay had been for a week, which to be honest was more like a holiday. The novelty of rubbish tips on nearly every corner, cows grazing in the road (and the rubbish tips), beggars pestering us at every bar (until the locals told them to scoot) and trying out my schoolgirl Russian on the locals (who spoke only that or Albanian) had made it a fairytale stay of unusual food and beautiful scenery. It was a whole new world of sights and sounds that few visitors had experienced; hardly anyone had visited at that time and even the tiny number of foreign missionaries had nearly all gone home during the anarchy of the nineties, hardly any of them returning. We Brits were like heroes because of Tony Blair's decisive dealings with the Serbs during the Kosovo war, often being pushed to the front of queues and greeted by all as long-lost friends.

This next, month-long, sojourn was to be quite different as we were able to see much more of the country, experience much more of the culture and, crucially, suffer much more of the day-to-day hardship that the local population endured.

This was good because, after all, this was the whole point of staying for so long and we were determined to live just like the local population on the whole.

At that time there were no direct flights to Corfu Island outside of the holiday season so we flew to Athens, which was about £30 each way for each of us. We had arranged to stay in the little flat next to Lida's parents' apartment at a very reasonable rate (or so we thought at the time!) and stay for one night at a cheap hotel in Athens ready to set off on the bus journey to Saranda.

All went well until we got out of the Greek taxi at the international bus station a few miles outside of the centre of Athens. At that time Greek currency was still drachma and Dan gave the driver a 5,000 drachma note, the smallest currency we had. The driver gave him change for only 500 and insisted that was all Dan had given to him. No amount of arguing would change his stance and we were left with a gaping hole in our very limited resources. Later we discovered that this was a common practice in many areas, where the driver would switch the notes in his money bag and insist that the passenger was mistaken.

This was only the beginning of a very educational month culturally and socially. We were quite naïve I think and needed waking up to the realities of life outside of our British comfort zone as non-tourists. This was going to be extremely interesting.

The journey by bus from Athens to Saranda was much longer than we expected at around ten hours but we loved the scenery and the atmosphere on board; of course, some air-conditioning would have been nice but thankfully this was autumn and below highest possible temperatures. All the other passengers were Albanians returning home from visiting children who were working in Greece, or others who had been away from home on business or holiday. Travel between the two countries at that time was fraught with difficulties if you were Albanian and the Greek border guards at Karkavia were less than pleasant to them. The worst aspects of the journey for me were the toilets here. We knew what to expect from our earlier trips – a hole in the ground with ledges either side to place your feet while you squatted over said hole. I had already negotiated the ones at the restaurant where we stopped for lunch. In fact I was quite pleased with myself that I had managed very well and worn a skirt in preparation. That is until I saw a couple of girls in jeans come out looking none the worse for the experience. They were of course Albanian and well used to performing the gymnastics required to successfully complete the task in trousers!

However, nothing had prepared us for the portaloos at the Greek/Albania border. These were a series of yellow innocuous-looking boxes, similar to the ones at festivals or building sites in Britain. As unusual as the normal Albanian toilet might be it was always clean and flushed easily with running water. Not so these monstrosities.

Now my husband is no softy – he is from the Midlands and grew up in a large, happy, family on a council estate, and went to a secondary modern school. He and his mates would play out all day in the school holidays and weekends. His front street was their football pitch. People from his area of town are used to the rigours of life and he had grown up much less fussy and soft than me, often joking that I was a princess because of the fairytale *The Princess and the Pea*. In practical terms he was a hardy sort whereas I just balked at the discomfort of this new adventure.

He went to use the facilities at Karkavia but quickly retreated as soon as he opened a door to one of the yellow facilities. He has never fully described what he saw and smelt inside but he refused to use them and told me firmly not to even go near. Suffice it to say it had had lots of usage throughout the previous days and not been cleaned, and there was no running water inside. This experience, as unpleasant as it was, did not prepare us for the actual crossing over at the border however.

Everyone from the bus was herded into a small enclosure outside the passport control office where the border guards waited to examine each person's papers and let them through. Although it was much less than summer temperatures, which could easily hit 40 degrees Celsius (equivalent to 104 degrees Fahrenheit), it was still warm at around 30 degrees and the space was very confined. The more people they pushed into the area the more concerned we became that we would be crushed. Holding our British passports in the air we waved at the guards who, seeing the documents, realised that an international incident might embarrass the Greek state and they rushed in to extract us from the mass of people, ushering us through the border quickly and safely, not quite apologising, but less surly than before and definitely less rough than in their handling of the Albanians. Over the coming years we came to realise that there was no love lost between the two nations, a fact that had many causes in the history they shared and the numerous myths which surrounded their relationship.

We witnessed many instances over the next few years which spoke of the ongoing feud between these two peoples – at this border and the sea border at Corfu Island – but we also saw how the Lord was working to bring reconciliation and peace where once there had been enmity and hatred. We saw first-hand how the love of Christ can impact a nation as the Lord builds the Kingdom of God, how the gospel not only changes individual lives but spreads like a canopy over the communities around them, how the Church can have a huge influence on a nation's identity and society at large. Just as we have seen a tragic decline in the values of the Kingdom in our land, we saw the opposite in the Land of the Eagles.

One of the most wonderful was the marriage between the pastor of the Evangelical church in Saranda to a local girl just after we began our mission there.

Sotir had come from the Evangelical Church of Corfu, an independent fellowship of Christians on an island dominated by Greek Orthodoxy. They had planted the even smaller church in Saranda as part of their mission to the Albanian people. He met and married his lovely wife who became a vital part of the ministry and their church has grown into the vibrant Christian witness it is today. This marriage would have been unheard of in Albanian or Greek society as a rule; Albanian Orthodox women were more likely to be married to Muslim men in Albania as long as they were both Albanian. This marriage between Sotir and Bruna was just one example of the precious love of Christ overriding division and hatred, bringing reconciliation to the people through the growth of the Kingdom of God. There was to be an even greater and more costly example in years to come however; this was the story of one of the most shocking and public incidents to happen in Albania's recent history, and one which we were privileged to witness part of on one of our later trips.

Blood feuds have been a tragic part of Albanian history reaching back into time well before the last few centuries and infecting their culture and behaviour right up to modern times. During Communism every area of life was so strictly monitored and controlled that this practice, as with all Albanian culture (including local recipes, which were banned by the party!), was suspended. Sadly, after the fall of the Communist regime in the early 1990s it returned with even less structure and rules than before.

A feud would grow up between two families if a member of one was killed by someone in the other clan. This was usually involving men as women were rarely allowed out of the home anyway and never without a male relative. This was to prove unfortunate for any poor female who did venture out alone – if she was taken advantage of by a male it was seen to be her own fault. There was no such offence as rape.

When there was a killing the family who had been stricken would not rely on the criminal justice system or take revenge themselves straight away; they would wait until the son of the perpetrator grew up and kill him. This would then continue down through the generations in a never-ending cycle of death and hatred, sometimes for many years and countless losses. We have been told that the Albanian Mafia is one of the most brutal and feared in the world for this very reason; touch one member and you enter into this never-ending cycle of death and fear.

The incident we witnessed was at the start of the 21st century. A young pastor from a neighbouring town had come to preach at the Baptist church of Saranda, the fellowship of which we had been part from our first trips to Albania and the group with which we would work whilst we lived there and for many years afterwards.

He was actually there just a week before one of our visits, preaching at the morning meeting that week, and he and his family had returned home just a few days before we arrived. Imagine our horror on learning that the following

Sunday he had been gunned down and killed on his church steps in front of his wife, young family and whole congregation. His family had been involved in a blood feud for years and this killing was the next generational step in the continuing horror. Nothing, it seems, can stop this vengeful act and when his murderer's son grew up this would be his fate.

Jesus spoke often and fervently about mercy when He walked on Earth and He still speaks through His word to His disciples today about our attitude towards our enemies. Matthew's account of Jesus's life, in chapter five, makes this very clear and this is just one example of His teaching about our attitude and behaviour as His followers towards those who hurt us. We are told to love them and pray for them and to reach out to them with His love, but I have never seen this more strongly lived out than by the wife and congregation of that young pastor who took to the streets only days later to proclaim to all who would listen that they would not seek revenge.

On national television they witnessed to the love of Christ, forgiving their loved-one's killer and saying unequivocally that the feud would end there. As Christians they witnessed to Christ's love and grace and refused to continue this awful tradition. As this man's whole congregation walked the streets of their town, proclaiming God's love, his death took on purpose and his people found hope for the future of their country. As we watched this event unfold we were inspired and humbled by the amazing response of Christ's church and so glad that we stuck with the call of God on our lives all those years ago when things were far from easy, especially back in our early visits.

So, a month in this environment was a daunting prospect but we were somewhat prepared by the swindling

Greek taxi driver to expect difficult times. Of course, there were also many blessings in store and the first one was just around the corner. This turned out to be a surprising and large reduction in our rent for the month when we arrived at Lida's mother's home. Whether this was because of the shocked looks on our faces when we opened the door to our 'apartment' to find it was one extremely small bedroom with a toilet in the corner, behind a curtained alcove, or just God's providence after the drastic hole in our very limited resources after said taxi fraud, we will never know.

This month was the real test of our calling to work with God in Albania. Such a huge decision needed to be clearly proved and this stay was going to be the proving (or not!).

So much happened during the month and I can only pick out a few events, but the first time we went north to visit the capital, Tirane, remains forever in my memory. The trip itself was amazing, starting as it did at three in the morning and taking at that time around nine hours.

We set off with Stefan, who worked with Lida at the Lydia Foundation and was going to a United Nations conference in Tirane, and XHalal (pronounced Jalal) who was her driver. Exciting as this was it was also a little disconcerting to know that we, who had hardly any Albanian, had been entrusted to the care of these men who had little or no English. It was even more worrying as it had been explained to us that the early start was necessary because, although the rule of law had mostly been established in the cities and towns, out in the mountainous wilderness anarchy still prevailed and armed gangs roamed unimpeded at night.

We were reassured to know that we would not be harmed, that they were simply after our money. We had little of this and most of it alongside our passports had been left safely at home in our apartment in Saranda. It was only five dollars a night to stay at the missionary centre in the capital so we took a twenty-dollar bill and some loose change for food.

The drive was fantastic, through mountain passes, along winding roads, over high peaks and always with huge drops down the side of the car. We saw many tiny shrines at the edge of particularly sharp bends; later in our stay we asked Lida about these and learnt that they were memorials for those who had gone over the edge. I am eternally grateful that the language barrier meant that we did not know on that first trip.

We saw no bandits en route but every town and village was guarded by a couple of police officers behind sandbags, carrying an array of automatic weapons. Some sense of safety there then, but more so in the fact that we all sang praise and worship to the Lord in our own languages all the way to the capital.

Tirane: the capital of a once repressive totalitarian state which was so hardline the leader fell out with China and Russia. Now abandoned for free market economy (or rather post-Communist corruption and chaos) and barely a year after almost total anarchy, the city was a mess.

Piles of rubbish higher than many buildings were on every street corner, beggars were literally everywhere and markets had few goods other than basic foodstuffs.

We sped through the centre and arrived at The Stephen Centre, a missionary hub built by the Americans for all Christian workers in Albania to use for accommodation when in Tirane. As we passed through the doors it was a surreal moment because the inside of the integral restaurant was exactly like a McDonald's, complete with menu, red and white décor and snappily dressed staff. What a shock after the streets of a city resembling Addis Ababa during the Ethiopian food crisis!

The menu was totally American, burgers and chips included, and almost every other thing on the McDonald's list. This was rather a contrast to the cold green beans in olive oil, or bread and banana that we had been served up in Saranda. In fact, we had learnt to live on pasta with salad and not much else for the past weeks. Shops were few and far between and the markets had very limited fayre.

We tucked in like people newly rescued from a desert island, savouring Western cuisine and ignoring the anomalies all around us. It was slightly more difficult when we were taken to the hostel (or rather luxury hotel) attached to the eating place and saw the opulence to which the visitors were treated. However, when the Dallas-like drapes and fixtures and fittings had ceased to be quite a shock we enjoyed long, warm showers and washed all our clothes, including the ones we had been wearing.

We had not realised that we did in fact smell a little unsavoury after the hours en route and the previous weeks of having little or no running water on a regular basis. Strange how these miracles of modern Western living are so taken for granted in the UK and how difficult life becomes when the electricity and water are off for days at a time. (I used to wonder why Albanians kept their bathtubs full of water all the time until it became clear that that was going to be the only way to flush the loo!)

In the coming years Tirane was to become quite familiar to us because our work took us there on several occasions, sometimes by car and sometimes by the much longer (and less comfortable) bus. A few of these trips stand out as special and one in particular was life-changing.

Over the years since the first modern Christian missionaries had arrived, almost as soon as the country had opened up after Communism fell, there had been a steady growth in the number of believers in Albania. When the anarchy of the nineties arrived nearly all the foreigners had gone home, some because of the very real dangers at the time, some because their sending churches or organisations had insisted.

This meant that the indigenous Church had to become more self-sufficient. This in turn led to many more local pastors and leaders being needed and consequently the establishing of the Bible school in Tirane. We had the great joy on one of our trips to the capital to stay there during the rare winter visits we made to the north, travelling through mountain passes more akin to the Swiss Alps as the peaks were dusted with snow.

The Bible school was full of life and enthusiasm, the students being mainly young fresh converts who had accepted Christ very recently and had a hunger for His word. It was also quite an old building and absolutely freezing as February in the north of Albania is cold, and there was little in the way of heating,

As we sat in the sparsely furnished dining room we shivered in our coats, scarves and hats and leant over steaming cups of tea – the only heat source available. Breakfast was bread and jam, although when the students had discovered that it was my birthday they scoured the markets and appeared with bananas and a single flower. Their generosity and love were wonderful but what was overwhelming was the time of worship which followed.

Klodi and Megena, a young married couple who were later to become good friends, began by singing 'Happy Birthday' to me; Klodi was a really good guitarist and both of them had lovely voices. This then turned into a time of worship and, more significantly, intercession – not, as one might assume, for Albania and its people, but for England and its real need for spiritual awakening. We all knew that our country was in as much need of God's touch on every aspect of its national life as Albania and we wept over the state of our country together. We were humbled by this experience, realising more and more over the coming months and years that we had been sent there as much to learn as to teach, to be changed as to bring change and to understand our Lord more as much as to explain Him.

Our opportunity did come on a subsequent visit to pray for Albania with other Christians from all over the country when we went to the first National Day of Prayer for their country, organised by the Albanian equivalent of the Evangelical Alliance. The amazing thing about this, apart from the thousands of people who packed into the central square in Tirane, was the fact that the pastors and leaders who stood on the steps in the centre were standing in exactly the same spot that Enver Hoxha had declared that Albania was the world's first atheistic state. Glory to God! No longer was it an atheistic state; the Church was growing and thriving and increasingly led by home-grown Albanian pastors!

So may wonderful things happened on these trips that it would probably take a whole book to describe them, but this next one just typically describes our experience of the generosity and hospitality of the Albanian people.

We were travelling once more by car to the capital, this time with Lida who wanted to stop off in Fier, which was halfway, to see her sister and family. This journey would take half the day so we would arrive there around lunchtime – about four hours into the long mountainous route.

When we got there Lida's sister was delighted to meet us all and asked if we would stay for lunch, always an invitation in Albanian homes if one arrived anywhere near a meal time; refusing this type of hospitality was impossible and highly offensive to the hostess. Lida said we could stay and we gratefully tucked into the mixed bean stew her sister had prepared, whilst she and her two boys looked on. I did think it was strange that they did not join us, only assuming they had had their meal before we had arrived. We had a lovely time with them all, the boys especially relishing the opportunity to practise their English which had recently become taught in all schools from the age of six – they were probably around eight and ten. Entertaining English people was rare in those days in the northern villages so this was a great opportunity for them.

What we did not know until we got outside to Lida's car was that the meal we had just enjoyed, savouring every delicious mouthful, was their main meal of the day and that they now would not have one. When she told us, we were horrified, even though refusing the hospitality would have been offensive in the extreme, realising that those two little boys would now go hungry.

Fortunately we had a few portions of cold pizza saved from the previous evening to eat on the trip, so we rushed back into the apartment to give them to the boys who were delighted at this change in their menu.

During all the many times we have stayed in Albania, and especially when we lived there, we never got used to the incredible generosity of the people, often those with the least amount of material possessions. The richness in simple humanity put our Western consumerism into sharp focus and showed us one of the roots of many of the ills of our society. The love of things.

The Bible calls it the 'love of money' and highlights it as the 'root of all evil' – not money itself, which is obviously a necessary tool for the transfer of goods and services, but the love of this tool and all it can obtain.

The pursuit of stuff has become a disease in the overdeveloped West which, for many of us, has led to the neglect of those things that are truly important, such as family, friendship, community and of course God.

Even in the Church, amongst believers, getting better, bigger, more successful lives in terms of possessions and status have become a subtle but insidious influence on much of what we do. Our time of prayer in the Bible school on my birthday had focussed almost entirely on the addictive consumerism which is so much a part of all our lives that we rarely if ever think about it, let alone question it. Although we had made the decision to leave England behind for a while it was always there in our hearts. This was mostly because our children were there, but also because, whatever happened in the next few years, it was our home.

We were to have a second home, however, for at least the next year and when the time came to leave the safety and relative security of the UK with its NHS, welfare state, general rule of law, fairly affluent lifestyle and all the other comforts we had taken for granted for much of our adult lives it was quite a change. A Bulgarian pastor had given us some timely advice not long before this: 'Where God guides, He provides'. We were to find that to be so true throughout our sojourn in Shqiperia.

13. A New Life in The Sun

When we had decided this was God's calling, and that Albania was to be our home for a while, we knew He would provide for us but also that there was to be some input from us towards this provision. Tent-making we call it in the Kingdom – the example set by Paul the apostle in the missionary travels that he undertook 2,000 years earlier, some of which were in this same area.

We had saved up a bit, but the main income which we would have was to have been from the rent from our house in the UK. This was going to be tight but we wanted to live like the locals so our costs would be quite low. Flights were still quite cheap back at the start of the new millennium so we would be able to come over regularly to visit family, staying with Mum; because we had moved her down from Manchester to our home town so she and Roxy could look after each other we had a base to stay when on home leave. The kids were economically independent (the level of income from student loans was mind-boggling to me who had been a 'starving student' in the 1960s) and we had enough income to help Jacob out if his job faltered. To be honest we were still hoping he might come out to the Med to live and work in Corfu, which had been our plan A. We missed all of them, of course, but he was still my baby and the missing was on a different level. Add to this that we were sure he should be coming with us and this was the hardest part of leaving home.

Arriving as we did in May, the weather was pleasantly warm and we quickly acclimatised. All was well, or so it seemed, but within the first week there had been several surprises which could have really sent us packing back home if the Lord had not intervened. This was a true confirmation of His plan for us in the end; we didn't see it that way at first, it was only as His amazing sovereignty unfolded around us that this became apparent. He is faithful, He is so good to us, He is all powerful and He knows everything. He was about to prove it yet again.

Our first real shock on arrival was the rather unexpected surprise that the young Albanian pastor of the Baptist church of Saranda had left his post, his town and his country. He had gone back to America where he had been trained and prepared by the American church which had first started the one in Albania. As it turned out the preparation was not that effective. He probably found it so hard to go back to the lifestyle in early 21st-century Albania after the extremely affluent, comfortable life in the States. In any event he was not there and we were left with a difficult situation. We had left everything and everyone we loved back in the UK to live there as Petro (our young, now absent pastor) had asked us to come and work with the church to set up a children's work. He told no-one else in the leadership that we were doing this. Needless to say, this was now not going to happen.

The next major blow was the disappearance of our tenant back home. This person had signed up for a year's tenancy with the housing agent we had chosen to handle the rental of our property. This whole idea had come from our dear daughter Roxanne who suggested that we downsize our home to clear our mortgage and then live on the rent which we would get. A wonderful idea, only now we had no tenant and no way of funding our trip beyond a few months. Would this mean that we would be returning home before the summer with a resounding 'No!' to the test of whether this was truly a calling from God or just our overactive imaginations?

The third, and potentially most disastrous, event was the revelation that we could only stay in the country for 28 days at a time because we had to renew our visas at this regular interval by leaving Albania and returning through passport control. This would need to happen until we got our residency permit which, we were told, might take up to a year. Discovering this after we had been there for only a few weeks came as rather a shock. We were informed that a kindly local policeman would do the honours for us in exchange for a 'coffee' (a euphemism for a small bribe, probably around 10 dollars). Now although this would have been cheap, easy and quite normal in the culture of the time in Albania, we were not going to start our mission work by resorting to bribery, entering into the generally accepted corruption and breaking lots of local and federal laws in the process. We said that as Christians we could not do this but the locals thought we were just being 'English', which I actually thought was a compliment. This still meant though that in around two weeks we were going to be illegal aliens.

So how would our loving, gracious and all-powerful Father sort this out? Well, He did it, as always, in His time and in His ways and we just had to sit back and watch the plan unfold. There was nothing else we could do so it was not difficult. We felt that the whole thing, which we thought had been wonderfully organised by us, had been taken out of our control. It had. Such a great lesson!

Having events taken out of my control was something with which I had had quite a lot of experience since that night in 1978 when I had given my life to the Lord Jesus. He takes us at our word if we do this in sincerity and truth, taking over the mess that we have made and reworking our lives to resemble the way we should have been; He does this to give us His peace. This 'shalom', which means much more than just peace in the original Hebrew, is the fullness of healing which only God can bring about. He restores us to be more and more the way He meant us to be, the way He created us to be had we not been born into this fallen world and with our sinful nature.

The end of my marriage to the children's father had been the first major crisis which He took us through. The children and I were carried by His love and I was healed of so much through that and my subsequent marriage to Dan. The damage to my back and miraculous healing was another major challenge that resulted in a greater freedom and more love in my life than I could ever have imagined.

Every difficulty is His opportunity to make us better, to make situations better, and therefore to have better outcomes. Back in the spring of 2002 we should have realised this but I do not think we did; we just wondered what we were going to do next. This was not the first time He had some crucial life lessons to teach me, to teach both of us, and it would not be the last.

In quick succession the Lord brought about the solution to all of these events, and in ways we could not have predicted.

The first solution was almost immediate – it needed to be – and involved our agent finding a new tenant within days for our property back home. In addition to this we were going to benefit financially as the original person lost their deposit on the property because they had broken their contract; not for the last time were we glad we had employed a properly qualified person to take care of the legal details of our rental. This gave us an extra month's rent which came in very handy, paying the fee for this housing company. Our God is extremely practical.

The second answer to prayer, because of course we were asking for His help, also came within a short time and was in the form of a phone call from our dear friend Sue who was looking after our financial affairs in the UK.

Delighted to give us the news, Sue informed us that a benefactor had paid £1,000 into our bank account anonymously that week. This would pay for our transport, accommodation if we needed it, and other expenses each month to go over to Corfu and back in order to renew our visas. Tough, I know, having to spend a night every 28 days in a holiday paradise, but someone had to do it!

It was amazing, glorious news. We were stunned by it but still slightly bemused as to exactly what we were supposed to do with our time in this developing nation where we were now sure we were supposed to stay for the foreseeable future. One thing we were sure of, we were on a mission from the Almighty and not just on an extended holiday.

The answer for this came a little more slowly but just as surely over the next few weeks; when it came it was a complete surprise.

'Albanian TV!'

When I was a child, and for many years into adulthood, I had wanted to be famous. Rich and famous maybe, although the money was not really important. I just wanted celebrity status. If it had been in this millennium I would have longed to be on *Big Brother* or *Love Island* I guess; back then it was *Sunday Night at the London Palladium* and the endless supply of Hollywood extravaganzas that were on the telly.

Throughout my formative years there was always that need for recognition and, yes, applause. Perhaps it was because of the rejection that I had suffered or maybe it was just my insatiable need for approval. From the first time that I got up on stage at my Godmother's wedding and sang to a rapturous (and rather captive) audience to the many people who had clapped for me in the various bands, choirs, musicals, operatic arias and solo gigs that had been scattered across my childhood and adolescence, the audiences' responses were addictive and I wanted more.

Whether as an actress or a singer this was my ambition but the road to success in the musical arts is littered with people who never make it, because family support and tremendous self-belief are two very necessary elements in the climb to the top (or even the lower middle). Needless to say, I had little of the first – Mum was too busy just working to put food on the table – and even less of the second.

After my early attempt at self-destruction this became even more difficult to attain and I settled for second-best as an amateur, with the occasional paid booking. I actually read recently (probably on Facebook, that fount of all knowledge!) that the root of the word 'amateur' comes from the word love, or passion, and that there is no dishonour in a pursuit of any amateur activity. I had a real passion for music, singing in particular. That may explain why singing became so central to my life. I longed for acceptance and recognition and singing was my one talent and where I got most pleasure because people loved my voice. In that way I could imagine they at least did not hate me. Singing was in fact, I believe, what saved me from complete self-hatred. It probably saved my life.

When the Lord rescued me, He gave singing a whole new purpose. Wonderfully, my voice became a tool in His hands to bless Him and His people. Worship in song became my new outlet, delighting in the Lord musically, which I was sure He loved and which I came to see His people were blessed by.

Throughout the early years of my walk with Jesus this gift was used by Him in many ways, including ministering in fellowship meetings, leading worship, song writing and recording. When we first began our visits to Albania this was no different and we were so amazed at the church in Saranda's response to the music that we brought. This culminated in our being asked to bring over a band to lead worship for all the churches in Saranda to come together in an evening of unity.

This was a wonderful experience for all of us, eight people from all over the UK and beyond including the lovely Sue, now our local Youth for Christ Director. The team had a great time having input into the local community including the state-run orphanage. The worship conference was packed with Christians from around the whole area, bringing a great sense of unity and encouragement to all of us.

It also gave us recognition in the city – not the kind I had hankered after before I knew the Lord; no, this recognition made us known in the whole Christian community and beyond. Consequently, when we moved out there the stage was already set for the Lord's initial purpose and the subsequent plans which He had put in place when our plans had fallen apart. Sound familiar? This so often happens in the Kingdom of God. We plan, sometimes meticulously, but He has different plans and they are always so much better!

It was at this event that we had come to know the new young pastor of the Baptist church of Saranda. He was preaching there and it was this event which had introduced him to Dan and I and given him the idea to invite us to set up a children's work for the church, giving us a real purpose for our mission. Sadly, it was this same young pastor who had left not long before we arrived, leaving us without work to begin our life in Albania.

This event was going to be used by the Lord for a completely different purpose, fulfilling my lifelong ambition to be famous and giving us both plenty to do in our first few months in the city.

Every year the tourist office of Saranda looked for new and interesting ways to build up the tourist industry, giving the local economy a much-needed boost and providing employment for many local residents as this industry grew. Our very good friend and brother in Christ, Fatos, had become quite successful in the previous few years in this industry. He had built a small hotel in the mid '90s when the visitors had started to trickle into the country after the fall of the Communist dictatorship. Over the years this had expanded and he had added a block of apartments on his land, one of which we now rented. In the next decade he would add a car-hire business, a currency exchange and an Albanian Evening in a local restaurant (including local cuisine, music and traditional dancing). There was even a 'Safari' in recent years, touring the whole region in Land Rovers, snapping the local wildlife on film, not to mention his most recent foray into yachting with his Israeli partner.

Fatos had, therefore, many contacts in the local government, especially the local tourist endeavours. When he heard that we were to have some time on our hands he immediately got us involved in the concert which was to be the event of the summer. Local singers, many of them professional, from all over the district had been booked to perform at this and Fatos somehow entered me into the programme – I am not sure how as I was the only non-

Albanian who would be singing, and I had no language to speak (or sing) of at the time!

The director of the theatre was a worship leader in the Baptist church and a good friend of Fatos, who in fact was good friends with almost the whole population of the city. Our nickname for him over the coming years was the 'Fresh Prince' of Saranda but he had no idea what that meant.

The theatre director was also the main organiser of the summer tourist concert, and an accomplished musician who was prepared to train me in the songs which I was to perform, even taking me through the gruelling rehearsal sessions needed to bring me up to professional standards. One of the songs, an aria from Bizet's *Carmen*, was actually in Albanian, a language of which Dan and I had only begun to scratch the surface. This did not faze the director and, to be honest, was not difficult to learn as the notes and the words sort of come as a package when memorising music. Our dear daughter, who had come over for her first holiday in Saranda not long before the concert, pointed out that I should find out what I was singing. 'You might be singing "I'm a little prostitute!"', she quipped. As it turned out she was about right!

Another song was from that most amazing animated account of God's deliverance of His people *The Prince of Egypt*, entitled *When you believe*. This was thankfully in English but was to be a duet with a young girl of 17 from the orphanage who had a beautiful voice and a very difficult past. Bruna had been placed in the orphanage as a young child when her widowed mother had remarried – a common practice in Albanian culture as the new husband would not take on the care of any children from the biological father as they were not his 'blood'. This was a difficult choice for a woman who had been left alone in serious economic and social difficulty, her options were few and perilous in those troubled times. As a result of this Bruna lost virtually all support or even contact with her family. To all intents and purposes this meant she was an orphan but whose mother still lived in the city. Understandably, she was a deeply troubled teenager who found any relationships difficult and trusted no-one.

We must have spent hours and hours on the songs, learning, polishing, rehearsing and repeating until we were ready to join the highly professional band which was to accompany us. Rehearsals with these musicians also took many hours but in the end the results were excellent. At the same time Dan was kept busy beginning the necessary work of building up resources, actually making many from scratch, ready for our new plan of action to begin children's work ourselves in the complex where we lived, trusting in the Lord to gather the participants to us.

We had been given a language tutor who was a retired teacher and began our twice-weekly lessons. Unfortunately, this lady proved to be both very expensive and totally unsuitable as she bombarded us with the Albanian language with little or no English to help. As we both found this regime extremely difficult, and therefore made little or no progress, we stopped these sessions after only a few weeks, even though this risked offending the locals. We quickly changed to a young high-school student who drilled us mercilessly in grammar and vocabulary but was an excellent coach and we soon made some progress. Amelina became a good friend over the next twenty years and she and her younger sister, Ansa, often met with us on our subsequent trips to the city.

The first few weeks passed rapidly, the temperature soared, and the date of the concert drew nearer. Our darling daughter Roxy had come over on holiday and we were excited to celebrate her milestone birthday with her. It was great to have her there as she was always so supportive of our work in Albania. I was also excited that she would be able to come to the concert on the small island out in the bay which was our stage for the evening. This was reached by a narrow walkway and gave the best possible venue for the whole of the promenade to be able to watch and listen to the music. The band was wonderful and we were well rehearsed.

The evening arrived and it was still quite nerve-wracking as we walked the short distance from our apartment down to the seashore. We passed through the milling crowds of locals and tourists, some of them from other parts of Europe or even the States, but nothing prepared me for the sight of the television crews and huge pantechnicons full of equipment next to the shoreline. No-one had told me that the concert was to be televised and transmitted all across Europe. Yikes! I found it very scary but the poor young singer from the orphanage was terrified. She just could not face the cameras, this presumably being the prime reason why we had not been told but, whereas my solution was to pray quietly for help, hers was to bolt. She could not, would not, sing and rapidly left the area altogether.

When you believe from *The Prince of Egypt* is a wonderful duet, sung by many great stars who have made it their own. The pivotal word here is duet – and now I was to sing it on my own.

Miraculously both this and the aria in Albanian went well, as did all the other performances by the local singers, and the whole evening was an amazing experience and a great success. I did get a telling off from the new pastor of the Baptist church, who came storming down to the seafront with his family, annoyed that they had only found out about the televising when they saw me on their own TV at home. Dan and I tried to explain that we knew nothing of this until the few minutes before the event, eventually receiving their approval and applause. Our dear daughter kept my feet firmly on the ground by teasing me constantly about my appearance on 'Albanian TV' – not a complimentary term as much of it at that time was news reports and old Norman Wisdom movies. This teasing was not a bad thing though as, for the first and thankfully only time in my life, I had fans who followed me about wanting my autograph.

The positive side to this fame was that it gave us a much higher profile in the city. We were interviewed by the local press who wanted to know why we had come to live in their country. So we told them. We told them that the Lord had told us to come. We told them that it was His love for the Albanian people which had caused us to leave our home and family back in the UK and work with the local Christian community to bring the good news of Christ's death on the cross in our place. It was His love for them that caused us to work and pray for improvements in their daily lives and especially for some of those who were the most marginalised in their city.

Following the concert Dan was asked to meet with the head of tourism who wanted his advice on making the city more attractive to foreign tourists, of which there were so far only a few. The Albanian authorities did not want to go the way of mass tourism; they had seen what the likes of Tui and Thomas Cook had done to Greece and Spain and wanted none of it. They did, however, see the economic benefits of some wealthier visitors, seeking to improve the environment to persuade them to return for longer stays than the Greek-run day trips from Corfu. This only swelled the economy of Corfu and did little to help the local businesses and population.

This was pretty easy for Dan to outline. We had often spoken about the general state of the city, which was dilapidated to say the least. There were also some much more serious issues that would greatly impede the progress of foreign tourism and made the lives of the locals much less pleasant.

To rid the city of the huge, rat-infested rubbish tips which sat unpleasantly at every major junction would be a good start, he advised, and when I say huge think the contents of a full bin lorry! To stop the unsupervised grazing of local cattle in these and other sources of food left lying around would be another great step. These animals wandered about with complete freedom throughout the year and seemed to have no problem feeding from the rubbish. Needless to say, we never drank locally produced milk (we had been advised not to do so before we left England as the local cows often had TB or brucellosis). English, German or other European guests were just not going to cope with this like the Albanians and would also appreciate swimming pools in the local hotels as they were not so used to swimming in the sea.

Also, he suggested, the beaches might not be littered with large amounts of refuse if there were a few rubbish bins dotted about and the addition of a tourist office complete with maps of the area would help a lot.

Dan, in his typically efficient and organised fashion, had put these ideas into a detailed written report, and we were amazed and delighted to see that over the next few years all of his suggestions were implemented. Tourism did indeed gradually grow and the economy alongside improved dramatically. Hotels opened, many of them complete with pools, all across the city and the visitors not only came but eventually many bought apartments which were to spring up all over the region during the next few decades.

This contact with local government gave us even more credibility with the local orphanage, which we had visited on some of our previous trips, bringing aid to the children in many forms including toothbrushes and toothpaste. Now the director welcomed us with open arms and asked us if we would do some teaching as the private English lessons which many other students had access to were just not available to his children. Dan and I therefore began our children's work at this orphanage and spent every Sunday or Saturday afternoon teaching English to around twenty students. We did not know it at the time but this work was to continue for the next twenty years in one form or another. We also began our Pocket Money project, which was to give each child a small but regular amount of money every week to buy sweets, comics or even basic essentials that those with no family could not afford. Friends in the UK who had visited the orphanage were more than happy to donate the small sums necessary and this project continued long after we left, administered by our trusted friend Fatos.

We had begun to have an impact on the lives of the people around us. Our community had felt the influence of the Kingdom of God through the people of God yet again and we were humbled to think that He might use us in some small way to improve people's lives. We were becoming part of the Baptist church who had welcomed us with open arms, despite them not knowing that we were coming. I became part of the worship team and Dan was given responsibilities by Lida, our original contact in Saranda and member of the church, for practical work that her NGO was doing at the orphanage. We were getting busier and busier.

The Lydia Foundation was and is a Dutch charity which had been actively working in relief and development work in Saranda since the 1990s. Lida was the director and driving force behind much of its work and during the Kosova war in 1999 had been instrumental in catering for the needs of several thousand Kosova refugees who had fled the conflict. As a volunteer with this organisation Dan was able to work with the orphanage in many ways, all of which again improved the life of the children.

When we first went there the lives of these children was miserable because, although it was a state-owned and funded children's home, the post-Communist world left much to be desired; as with many of these countries corruption was rife and this institution was no exception. We saw first-hand how this impacted the lives of these children, from gifts which we had brought them disappearing to the homes of staff to blatant fraud by the director.

The post of director was a political one – if the party which appointed you lost the election you lost your job, so there was little security there. Also, I do not imagine it was well paid as all work which did not involve physical labour was paid a pittance during Communism. Intellectuals were kept down in Hoxha's day, as in all communist states; they are the ones who cause trouble after all. Sadly, this had continued long after the fall of the Communist regime. Teachers in the early 2000s still earned less than a waitress and hardly enough to cover the rent of a family apartment.

We were appalled to see the rat-infested rubbish tip at the orphanage gates grow larger and larger as the summer approached and were happy to give the director a reasonable sum of money to have it taken away by lorry. Only later did we discover that he had asked for, and received, the same amount from several other people. They were other visitors or aid organisations from abroad and we often shared information. Needless to say, we were much more cautious after this.

Corruption was rife: the teachers' private lessons, the 'buying of coffee' for police and the paying of bribes to have building work approved. Everywhere we were surrounded by this and the local people were trapped in the acceptance of this to get anything done. Gradually though, as we stood against this and resisted the temptation to join in (it could have made life so much easier in the short term) we began to see a shift. One day Dan was in the internet café and got chatting to a group of students who were part of the 'Mjaft' movement, a group of young people committed to change. They were tired of their corrupt society and were working and campaigning to see change. Mjaft means enough in Albanian and they had had enough of the system which ruined their chances of advancing in so many fields. Again, we saw the influence of the Lord and His Kingdom on the life of the nation.

The most dramatic example of the shift in the nation's spiritual state which we witnessed was on the day of prayer for Albania in Tirane where we joined thousands of other Christians (most of them Albanian) to pray for their country. It was led by Albanian pastors and took place in Skanderberg square, right in the centre. The total area is about 40,000 square metres and it was full to overflowing. On the steps of this central area of the city the pastors declared that Albania belonged to Jesus. On these same steps a few decades earlier the Communist dictator, Enver Hoxha, had declared Albania to be the world's first atheistic state. Not anymore!

We were privileged to be a tiny part of God's restorative work in this nation, however small that may have been, and often we saw our role as simply supporting the local church and bringing relief and development to the larger community.

As we began to develop the kids' clubs, which eventually were to take up so much of our time and energy, we also began to be able to communicate more and more with the locals but still our need for interpreters was obvious. Two young people from the local Evangelical church came to our aid. Ansa was only 12 at the time (our Albanian teacher's younger sister) and Jonida had just finished high school. All were from poor backgrounds but wanted to help the local children and us. They literally were a Godsend and became part of our extended household on 'Klubi' nights.

'Klubi' was the term we all used for the children's house groups we began in our apartment towards the end of our third month in Saranda, after the height of the summer season and near the beginning of the school term. At first this was one night a week but by the end of our stay we had four a week, plus the work in the orphanage, seeing over a hundred children every week. With the preparation and church activities we were working around 40 hours a week but were never exhausted, because God did provide in every way.

Each club night we had singing, in Albanian, a Bible story and prayer and then the children ate snacks while they coloured in pictures from the story. We always had a gospel message and were delighted to see a few of the children and one of our volunteers come to Christ while we were there – not hundreds but a few who became active members of the local church and were discipled by Albanians. We always say that even if only one person was saved it would have been worth the stay there and that only the Lord knows the effect of our serving Him in obedience. We needed to remember that in the years which followed when the doubts came – as they always do – with the thought that we were complete failures or that we should never have gone in the first place. All He really asks of us is obedience and trust. We are both still learning this.

Over the next twenty years we would spend much of our time and energy in Albania, even after our return to live in the UK and it sort of became our second home. The people were very dear to us and the church was our other fellowship. Of course, we were home for Christmas that first year away, staying at Mum's and sharing this holiday with all of our children. Our trips home to England were wonderful, we had missed the children so much, and the first year sped by. We did not know how long we would be living abroad but after a little more than a year we needed to return to England permanently and this was to happen suddenly.

14. Homecoming

My darling daughter had a tumultuous time when Dan and I spent our 18 months living in Saranda, and although she was extremely supportive of our mission there, had some struggles of her own. We had moved Mum down to our home town so they could look after each other while we were away but that did not always work out. Roxanne experienced first- hand some of her Gran's more difficult personality traits. This was heartening in a way because none of the children had ever witnessed the way she could behave but it was hard for my darling girl to cope with, loving her Gran as she did.

It is not an understatement to say that when we came back to the UK for her graduation Roxy's announcement that she was having a baby floored us. We were happy to hear that she had found her faith in God again and excited at the prospect of our first grandchild's arrival but perplexed in the extreme. How could we support her in her wonderful decision to keep this baby, even though she was going to have to face the future alone? After much thought we decided we would come home a short time before the birth and that I would stay for three months while Dan went back after a few weeks to continue our work out there.

How short-sighted we were. There was no way she could have coped with that, and we finally woke up to the reality of the situation when the housing people offered no help with housing beyond seven weeks in a mother and baby hostel ... and then nothing. In the end we were left with no choice but to leave Albania five months before the baby was due without housing or any income, or the least idea what we were going to do about either; no jobs and a tenant who had only just signed a sixth-month tenancy agreement on our house made both problems seem insurmountable. You would think we had learned by then that no problem is insurmountable to Almighty God; I think I have come to the conclusion that I am a slow learner.

Once more we had plans but God had an entirely different agenda, one which I struggled with to be honest. My pride was hurt, because I saw myself as a failure – but that was nothing new. There was little to show for our time abroad, or so we thought, and we had spectacularly failed as parents apparently as we set about rescuing our little girl from the situation that she was in. We were of course still being cared for by this extraordinary Father who had known that this was going to happen and made provision for us all; this was, as always, part of His sovereign plan and would only work out for our good and His glory.

Our home church in the UK had recently begun to support us financially and when we returned to England continued that support for several months, so we did not starve. We were not eligible for social security as we had lived outside the UK for over a year so this was God's provision. As for housing, a wonderful family in the church had a self-contained flat at the top of their spacious house and housed us in it. Then the people who had rented our house understood the serious need we all had for a home, especially the coming baby, and vacated the house within a month. Once more the Lord took charge and made a way where there seemed to be no way. Despite all of this I was feeling bewildered and unsettled by this sudden shift in our plans. Add to this I had just entered into the difficult upheaval of menopause, with all the physical, emotional and mental challenges that this brings.

More recently I have come to understand why it takes me so long to process change and the bigger the upheaval the longer it takes; I have learnt so much since we returned to England about my mental health issues and understand why so much turmoil hit me at that time. Thankfully there has been much healing since then, healing which is available to all who have suffered trauma in their past; healing that is available to you, in Christ.

To me the future looked bleak as we struggled to find work, pick up the pieces of our lives and prepared for the prospect of a new baby in the house. Dan was able to return almost at once to work in the supermarket where he had worked before we left England and supply teaching was fairly readily available. My trust in God wavered as I struggled to come to terms with this massive change and my faith wobbled as this and the trauma of the menopause began to bite. What none of us knew was the amazing set of circumstances which would work together for good, even in this.

The day of baby's birth drew near and God was at work in us all, refining and preparing us, and when she was born this baby girl was the light of all our lives. Tired in the extreme and stretched to the limits we all rose to the challenge and in so many ways it was a delight to share in the whole event. We hardly gave a second thought to Dan's small medical problem which that Christmas and just a couple of months before baby day seemed to have been sorted out quite simply. It did seem strange that he was as tired as Mother and Nana, after all he slept soundly through every night feed and went to work all day to a much less tiring regime than new parenting! The reason for this became apparent when we discovered the problem had not gone away and a few weeks after the birth it returned with a vengeance.

A simple scan revealed the awful truth – Dan had cancer and would require almost immediate surgery for there to be a good outcome. This was a terrible shock to me, still wavering in my trust of the Lord, but Dan just went straight back to work after the diagnosis and got on with life. I, great woman of faith, went to my dear friend Sue's house and planned the colour of funeral cars on the way.

When I arrived in her kitchen, in tears, she told me straight away not to start planning the funeral – a bit late as I had already started that in the car on the way over. Sue was and still is a woman of faith whose own difficult circumstances had only served to make her stronger and more consistent in her trust in God. She prayed with me and helped me to see that He was still in control and that I should have hope in His goodness. Stopping off at the local budget supermarket I bought the king-size duvet set that we had recently decided was needed as Dan always pinched the covers and left me frozen in the middle of the night now that we were back in the much colder climate of England. He was going to survive and this was going to be needed!

So, I went home much encouraged and over the next few months the Lord helped us both to trust Him for the outcome. Our lovely daughter had organised a weekend away for us just before the surgery, a much-needed time together to distract us from it all. Our dear friend Libby told us that God was taking us through the 'Valley of the shadow of death' but that we must not camp there. Slowly we had our sights lifted from the circumstances to His glory and when the treatment had finished and the outlook was very positive, we all praised God for His gift of healing. Roxy has always said that her baby girl in fact saved Grandad's life; this is probably partly true as he would have had little hope of a diagnosis so quickly had we still been in Albania. Even if he had, by the time we had got back home for treatment it may well have been too late. Now, over nineteen years later we praise the Lord for His wonderful gift of Dan's continued good health.

We missed Albania very much. That first year back we were too occupied with baby and cancer treatment to even visit, but neither of us realised that our work there was far from finished. This developing nation had become our second home, as said earlier, and it was to continue to be a large part of our lives for many more years to come. It was not that we had little to do; our first grandchild was followed by five more and these wonderful children have kept us busy, enriching our lives far more than we could have imagined. We both went back to work and I found teaching more rewarding than ever, but God's plans cannot be stopped and He still had plans for us over in the Med.

15. The Jonida Foundation

In the early 21st century there had been many improvements made in the lives of the average person in southern Albania. Stable, if still corrupt to some extent, the state generally cared reasonably well for the population if they could not work, although by living standards here and in the rest of Western Europe most of the population would have been seen as living in extreme poverty. The state pension was a pittance, literally a fraction of the one that we have here in the UK, and people who had to try to live on this tiny amount (probably around five pounds a week when a loaf of bread was around 50 pence!) relied on children to support them. If they had no children they would sit on the sea front each evening with a set of bathroom scales or packets of seeds. Locals and tourists would pay a small sum to check their weight or buy produce and this would supplement their finances; far less humiliating for them than outright begging!

The starvation once seen in the far north had abated and the towns and cities seemed much safer. In the villages the school system was far better although much of this had been established by charities.

Few had cars, very few owned their own apartments and all lived a simple life, which in most cases was hand to mouth. Development was slow but tourism was growing and with it more secure employment. We were not seeing the abject desperation we had seen in the 1990s.

The Church was doing a good job of supporting the very poorest families and the Bread of Life scheme run by several fellowships made a big difference. This literally provided the basic food for many destitute families through the donations of better-off members of the fellowships and foreign visitors. Families who had sent adult children abroad to work, more often than not at great risk and illegally, were seeing the benefit of that investment as large amounts of their wages came back into the Albanian economy. Many apartments were renovated or even built using this money as children earned enough to send relatively large amounts to their parents back home.

Tourism was growing as investment was made into local building projects so there were far more jobs for local workers who no longer needed to go to Greece and Italy to find employment. With this growing affluence there came many benefits but also many drawbacks – a casino was built, a strip joint sprang up and night clubs opened for the first time. People had more materially than they had ever had but lost the simple uncomplicated community life which we had once shared where friendship and family were all-important, where we had learnt to value the simplicity and richness of community life without the trappings of modern society.

One group of people who had benefited to some extent from this improvement in lifestyle were the children who lived in the orphanage. This 'children's home' was anything but a home when we first visited but had seen more home comforts, such as better beds, decoration of concrete walls, staff who had some training in child care and directors who were far better equipped to run such an institution and far less corrupt than their predecessors.

As mentioned earlier, these children and young people, ranging in age from around four to sixteen, were rarely orphans but had been taken into care because their parents could not afford to look after them or their mother had remarried and the new husband would not take them. This was a rare but horrible occurrence in Albania; grandparents would take the unwanted children if they could, but most widows would wear black for many years after their husband had died, thus fending off prospective suitors rather than lose their children in this way.

Sadly, the local government (think county council and borough council here in England) did little to fulfil their obligations to these institutions which existed in other areas of the country too. Central government provided buildings, staff and basic foodstuffs. Consequently, the children were missing out on some rather essential provisions. This included toiletries, school clothes and sufficient meat and milk in their diet; crucially there was no provision of supplementary tutoring at home which was absolutely necessary if they wanted to make progress.

In many of our early visits to Saranda we, and the teams who had come with us, would bring toothbrushes and toothpaste, essentials which were not provided by the institution! We had brought school clothes, stationary sets, rucksacks and other treats for the children. In the earliest times we gave them to the staff until we discovered that most of the goodies went home with them for their own children; later we gave all such gifts directly to the children. I still remember the delight of the children when we brought new school rucksacks for each of them, made possible by the team of volunteers who had come over with us to run a holiday club for the orphanage one summer. These holiday clubs were a special time for both the teams who came and the children who enjoyed them. School holidays were long and boring for this group of children who, at the time, saw little of the benefits of living in a holiday paradise. They rarely saw the outside of the orphanage walls and only in more recent years were organised trips to the beach provided, with staff supervision. Even more recently the glorious outings to

Corfu were laid on, probably funded by the American charity which had taken on so much of the children's care.

This large American charity had begun to tackle the food issues initially by providing this directly to each state-run orphanage in Albania through the generous donations of Christians back in the States. This was administered locally by trusted members of the local church so that the money did not just disappear into the pockets of some official on the way to the orphanages. So corrupt were many of the officials in many government departments that millions had been misappropriated since the country had first opened up in the 1980s. This forced major donors such as the European Union or investors in tourism and property to bring in their own workers to build roads, bridges or apartments rather than see funds disappear.

As mentioned earlier, we had also experienced this on a small scale so we were fairly well placed to set up a relief project which would work and this we set about doing once Dan was fully recovered and Roxy and our granddaughter, Grace, were settled with their own little family in their own home many miles from us.

This was the birth of The Jonida Foundation and was to have a far bigger impact on our lives than we ever imagined when it began. This small, insignificant charity was the obvious way for us to continue the aid work in which we had been involved with the community but what we did not know at the time was the difference it was going to make to our ongoing involvement with more of the Lord's work in Saranda.

Why 'The Jonida Foundation'?

When the Lord sent us to Saranda as missionaries our primary aim had been to see many come to a living and powerful relationship with Jesus. This was our primary aim but God showed us that His influence on the people we lived amongst, their communities and the improvement of their lives was also essential. Of course, I thought our work would lead to dozens, if not thousands, being swept into the Kingdom of God. My battle with pride was still in its infancy and my expectations were probably based on reading too many books of victorious living and endless accomplishments that the early part of my Christian life had been littered with. Then the reality hit. There were a few who we saw directly give their lives to Jesus but one particular young lady made a great impression on us as a volunteer at our kids' clubs. She became a believer, she told us, directly through our work there and went on to serve and follow Him. She was Fatos' cousin and her name was Jonida.

The Jonida Foundation became, for the next almost twenty years, His way of showing us how we could still be involved in His work there as our trustees joined with Dan and I to serve the people of that nation still, this time at a distance for most of the time.

For the last 44 years I have walked with Jesus and I have come to realise that He never wastes anything from our lives, past or present, in the work of His Kingdom. From my having learnt Russian at school, which had been very handy before we had learnt any Albanian in a post-Communist state, to Dan's amazing administrative and craft skills, all were used to great effect in our kids' clubs. Now we were to put many of these skills alongside the other talents of our team and produce some amazing fundraisers.

For me obviously concerts were key. We have so many talented friends, from magicians to dancers, from bands and duos to soloists, and these just kept coming and entertaining throughout. Afternoon teas in the summer were also popular, especially those hosted by our dear friend whose garden bordered a cricket pitch.

All-day breakfasts, courtesy of a chef friend, Dan's incredible long-distance walks and even my sponsored walk of 1,000 miles (over a year I hasten to add) all added together to raise tens of thousands of pounds over the years. So many volunteers, so much support, many hours of work and fun and such great results.

<u>So, what was the purpose of the Jonida Foundation?</u>

I have just been looking at a post from a Facebook 'friend' which is likely to see me sliding down into a negative sloth of despond; in it he talks of many healings, souls saved and other miracles every time they visited homes in their mission field long ago. Always tending to look on the less than bright side of life I just find myself comparing this to our experiences and feeling, as usual in most areas of my life, a bit of a failure. Dan is so good at talking me out of this state of mind, especially where our wonderful children are concerned (World's Worst Mother badge displayed!) and I am getting better at talking myself out of this negative mindset.

In this case though even I can see what an impact the Foundation has had on many people and the way it has kept us connected for so long to our second home, Albania.

In any developing economy education is, as always, the key to improving individual lives and families. Ultimately, it is the way that any society improves the aspirations and skills of its people. Education that is universally available can only improve the lives of all a country's citizens if it is fair and run with integrity. Sadly, the education system in Albania was at the time of our involvement far from fair and, in many cases, lacking in integrity.

Even in the years after we had left the country, for some – the children of the rich mainly – any qualification could be obtained by bribing those in schools and universities who were able to 'fix' the results. For many others in the growing number of slightly better-off families, the burgeoning middle classes, the way to obtain good results was slightly more complicated.

Because teachers were still paid badly, even in more recent times, they had to supplement their income by teaching students privately after school and at the weekend. A teacher's pay would barely cover the rent on a small apartment, where most of the population still live. Obviously, unless two people were working there was nothing left for the rest of life's necessities.

Many had no other choice but to offer private tuition in their specialist subject in the evenings or Saturdays. These private 'courses' were the only way for most teachers to survive and, for the students, a good way to improve their results. Most parents would work hard to enable their child to attend these; the fees were quite reasonable for the most part, the teachers putting in the extra hours to help their students to succeed.

There was another less noble type of arrangement however which ensured that the student passed the relevant subject without too much effort. Some educators would guarantee the success of an individual if private lessons were paid for, ensuring that the student gained the marks needed whatever their exam paper or essays contained.

We saw this at high school level and heard awful testimonies from university students who had been told to enclose money with each piece of work submitted to ensure they passed that particular professor's standards. One friend had complained to the principal of her university about this practice only to be told that this was accepted by him (presumably because he too was benefiting from the fraud).

Not all education staff were corrupt however. While I was living there the head of English in the city approached me to help some of her English teachers in their profession and I was impressed with their dedication and aspirations for their students. Some of these older students came to me as I ran an Oxford English course and were pleased when I assured them that the tests involved in this could not be passed by cheating. They wanted some qualifications which would be recognised by the rest of the world as most Albanian ones were not, for fairly obvious reasons! This left many young people feeling hopeless about their future and the most talented left their homeland to pursue their future in other countries. Sadly, few ever returned.

There was nothing we could do but pray and trust that the Lord would reform this institution as He brought His influence to bear more and more as His kingdom advanced. We saw our small role in this to help the children of the orphanage to access the kind of education available to other students. To this end we set up a teaching programme in the children's home of Saranda.

We had many friends in our home town who had supported us during our stay in Albania, in fact many of them had visited us over there or come with us on team visits.

Some of these dear people became trustees and supporters of the charity which was to continue to be the bridge between here and Saranda which I had seen in that dream all those years before.

We began by organising a variety concert at our local arts centre, a coming together of local talent, which provided the funds to begin this work. For nearly two decades we worked with a wonderful core of supporters to establish the teaching programme that changed the lives of these children. There were many more concerts, Dan's amazing sponsored walks which took several days and covered many miles, afternoon teas, all-day breakfasts, Christmas fairs and too many other events to even remember. We were also blessed to have a group of regular monthly supporters whose direct debit payments enabled us to plan for the future on a much more long-term basis.

Once more we visited the orphanage and took aid to the children and because there had been a change of director – this time a trained educator who really seemed to put the needs of the children first – we began by asking her what the children's greatest need was.

Their greatest disadvantage was the lack of educational support. She told us they suffered so much because they did not have parental input in every aspect of their lives of course, but the need for help in their learning was immense. To begin with, the smallest ones, only five or six when they entered the care system, needed lots of help emotionally and psychologically and the state had begun to recognise this, supplying professional help in the children's homes. Physical needs were being met by charities for the most part, but education had been neglected. Some children could barely read and write and others just could not engage in the school system.

Our first intervention therefore was to set up a course for children who were new to the orphanage and who were struggling in school. With the help of Fatos once more and the full support of the director, we funded this in the first few years of the Jonida Foundation at the children's home, employing a local teacher to run it. We also supplied stationary and other material goods which the children lacked.

The success of this meant that these children were able to settle into school and reap the benefit of classroom teaching, and once they did other children joined the course. There was a rolling, ever-changing group of mostly young children who were given the extra support needed to be fully integrated into the school system. There was no additional support in schools at that time for any kind of special educational needs. If a child would sit and be quiet in class, whether they could participate or not, they were allowed into lessons but that was the full extent of the system's provision in the early 21st century. Children who did not make progress for any reason quickly fell further and further behind their year group and would often be kept back a year which only added to their dysfunctional relationship with school.

Providing this extra help made a big difference to the children but it also had a major influence on the staff who were employed as 'teachers' by the state. These white-coated ladies usually sat around drinking coffee all day and seemed to have little to do with the children's education; they did not seem to relate to the children in many ways at all in fact. The presence of a professional teacher inspired them to get involved in the education of the children in their care to a greater extent, helping with homework and working with the children more often rather than just supervising them.

During our first few years as education providers we saw a real change in the culture within the children's home, possibly because of the influence of our and other charities' presence. Perhaps the local workers were inspired by the presence of professional teachers or perhaps they were just replaced, like the director, by people who genuinely cared about the children and young people in their care. Whatever the reason, and of course we saw this as answer to prayer, they became much more professional, much more involved in the lives of their charges and much more pro-active in their education.

During this extended length of time we had visited often, bringing teams over in the summer and gifts for the children whenever we could, often speaking to the staff and children about the lessons which The Jonida Foundation was providing. We even looked at the progress which the children had made and their subsequent performance in school whenever possible. We laughingly referred to this as our 'OFSTED' inspection but it was in fact the only way that we could be sure the money we had donated was being used effectively. Perhaps we were a little cynical and suspicious after our experiences in the past. We need not have been, the new director and her subsequent successors were totally different. The place had become a real home and the children's lives transformed.

When it became apparent that things had improved greatly and that the staff were now helping new entrants in their care to settle into school by giving them the support we had provided, the director came up with the next stage of classes which were needed.

Many of the older, high school students were showing great promise and some of them were ideal candidates for higher education. The American charity which had been involved in providing practical support for many years in all the state-run orphanages in Albania had set up a wonderful centre in Tirane where these gifted young people could stay and be enrolled in the university. They were bussed in and out of campus and supervised carefully by the staff to guard them from the people traffickers who often preyed upon Albanian young people – especially the girls. Horror stories were commonplace of girls who had left the orphanage at 16 disappearing into this abyss. Albania is still seen as the people trafficking centre of the world and many young girls are groomed by young men who promise them love, marriage, security and prosperity abroad. Our dear friend Lida had seen this happen to her beautiful fourteen-year-old daughter who had to go and live with friends in England to escape the clutches of one gang. This child was very vulnerable and attracted the attention of a criminal gang who assigned one of their young men to give her lots of attention.

If she had not escaped to a family in England the reality of what happens to these young girls when they run away with their new 'love' may well have developed and she would have found herself locked in an upstairs room somewhere in Europe awaiting a terrible fate with little hope of rescue.

As the work at the centre in Tirane developed we were tasked with a new goal by the director; the students from her institution had one major disadvantage – they could not participate in the private courses that most parents routinely provided in many of the core subjects and this showed when applying for higher education. It slowed their progress in school and impeded their success.

If we could fund more teachers who in turn could take small groups of older students to a better level in these important subjects then we could help some of them to get to university. This of course appealed to us as our initial thoughts when setting up the Jonida Foundation had been to fund university places for the orphanage young people. As the Americans were already doing this we were to act as a bridge, once again, for them to gain access to these degree courses.

During one of our visits to Saranda the director outlined this plan, which would obviously mean more money but would have a very positive outcome.

As we returned to the UK we and our team prayed for God's guidance and it seemed right to us all to pursue this new development; we did this with each new venture and challenge and He was always faithful to provide wherever He guided us. He always has been and always will be.

Over the next few years we employed various teachers, some retired some unemployed, to tutor students in maths, science and the Albanian language. These important subjects were essential to the students' prospects. Fatos would pay them from the funds which were raised in England and we continued to do our 'inspections' in order to assure our supporters that the money was well spent. We all thoroughly enjoyed the events which brought in most of these funds and the work involved seemed a joy as we could see the progress which the students made. In one wonderful visit we met up with a group from Tirane who had been recipients of The Jonida Foundation's tutoring. They were staying at the same small hotel as we were with their hostel leaders and we were told by these staff that 'our' students were the best ones to have come from any of the orphanages in Albania – a tribute to our teachers and The Jonida Foundation! In addition to this we were also able to fund several students in Africa on their journey through higher education through our contact with friends working in Burundi.

There was to be more to come as God opened up yet another exciting possibility during one of our stays in Saranda, where we continued to visit often several times a year. Of course, we kept a close eye on the progress of our students and our involvement with the church there never waned.

One of our dearest brothers in Christ was Bimmie who was the son of the first pastor of our fellowship in the city. He also was a doctor who had become a good friend when we lived over there and had developed into a real supporter of the Jonida Foundation. Whenever we were in Albania we were inspired by the work he was doing with the most disadvantaged especially after he took over as director of the Dutch relief charity that Dan had worked with in 2003.

In Albania in the past anyone who was physically disabled or had any kind of learning disability was completely ostracised by society. These people, many of them children, were kept hidden away in homes which were covered in shame because they were seen to be 'cursed'. This ancient practice was, sadly, still common in the first decade of this century, families being forced to care with almost no support for any relative who had complex and severe additional needs.

Bimmie, who was also a highly qualified ENT surgeon like his father, was about to revolutionise his culture by providing a day care centre where there was specialised care and therapy available. He also set up a speech and language programme for children who were struggling to communicate and had no support at all in school.

His centre employed physiotherapists and speech therapists amongst others and was funded entirely by charities which included the Jonida Foundation for a number of years. This work was so new and ground-breaking that we were privileged to be part of it but there was even more to come.

Through our involvement with Bimmie's work an opportunity opened up for us to pay for one-to-one support in the schools for children who were not able to access education because of their special needs. At first the teachers were unwilling to have another adult in the classroom; they could see no point in it and as long as the child was quiet and not disturbing the lesson there was no need. Eventually, after much lobbying by Bimmie, the first teaching assistant entered the educational system in the city and it was to bring steady progress. The teachers could see very quickly the difference that this made, particularly in the lives of the students. We were so happy to facilitate this but we were ecstatic when the school system began to employ TAs themselves. Once more the kingdom of God was having a dynamic effect on the society around us because of the work of His people.

Back at the speech therapy centre we once more had the opportunity to develop the work which the Lord was doing there. After our initial funding pledge, which would provide speech therapy for a number of students, we saw that there was one very important element missing. The children who were involved in this did not have the advantage of Makaton.

Many years earlier when Dan and I had worked at a special school which catered for students with speech and language difficulties we had both been fluent in Makaton, a sign language based upon a modified form of British sign language. This was used to augment speech and supported by a set of symbols used to replace written language. People with severe speech and language difficulties use Makaton to aid their communication, in some cases it being the only way they can express themselves.

The training that we had and the way Makaton was used made us absolutely sure Albanian therapists needed to have training in order to support their clients fully and the children needed this to aid their communication. But how was this going to happen when it was just not part of their experience?

The answer became clear when it seemed that the Holy Spirit was prompting us to do this ourselves. How was this going to happen when we both had employment here and our home was definitely not going to be rented out again? Also, our precious grandchildren had grown to six in number and were a very important part of our life in the UK.

This time though we were not going to leave our home country for an indeterminate length of time; this time we were just going on an extended visit.

Dan had been working at a local supermarket for more than twelve years and we had both been doing private tuition for some time. I had 'retired' from any permanent schools work early in order to look after Mum in 2012 but after she had gone home to be with the Lord in 2016 that role had ended.

Dan's employers had a sabbatical scheme which allowed employees to take up to three months unpaid leave in order to do specific activities. He asked for this time off and it was granted so off we went to stay in the Med again, this time for two months, with the support of friends in the UK who looked after our house.

Throughout my walk with Jesus I have experienced such great love from His people, we truly are a family, and across the world we are united in one bond, one body with one Head. Of course, there are times when things go wrong in the Church and when this happens it can be painful as in any family, but as with any other difficulty Romans 8 verse 28 holds true, God really does work everything together for our good if we love Him and are called according to His purpose. This is certainly true of where He places us in His Church. Without the support of the Body of Christ much of what we did in Albania would have been impossible, including this trip.

It was also true that it had been many years since we had both learnt Makaton and we were both very rusty. The Lord had this all in hand however and one day on one of my long walks through a local village I was amazed to see a sign pinned up on a lamp post advertising refresher courses in Makaton to be held in a local primary school over the sixth months prior to the time when we thought we might go. Such a great piece of provision and once more we were to see that indeed 'where God guides, He provides'!

We flew out in late May to be met by a well-organised Bimmie (unlike our longer adventure years earlier) who had arranged for us to sit in on speech therapy sessions but, more importantly, invited students and their families to meet us.

A wonderful group of children with mums, dads and grandparents came to learn about the Makaton course which we were designing. So many attended that we had to split into two groups which then came every week for our whole stay to learn this new language. I had written songs in Albanian, very simple songs to already familiar tunes, and we then added Makaton signing to these which Dan taught to the groups. We had such fun learning these songs and signs and each session was thoroughly enjoyed by us all, including the therapists who also came along.

Dan's special skill was creating Makaton symbols, which he had used extensively at the special school where he had worked as a classroom assistant. Now he was able to produce some of these in the Albanian vocabulary which would be most helpful, giving the speech therapists the opportunity to use them in their therapy sessions and create their own further down the road.

Again, we were able to see the Kingdom of God have a positive effect on the lives of the people around us and witness to Christ's love for them by our presence – and we were going to be much busier than we thought when we originally planned the adventure. Unknown to us our dear friend Fatos had more on the agenda for our visit!

For many years he and a small team of deacons had been leading the Baptist church of Saranda after Bimmie's father had retired from his position as pastor. The church would eventually have its own full-time leader from America (which would bring its own set of challenges) but for a few years these men had been overseeing the work and Fatos asked us if we would consider setting up and running two further groups while we were there.

The first was a ladies' group in the church which had really struggled and needed inspiration and I was asked to lead the group – a real delight as many of these dear ladies had been there when we lived in the city and worshipped at that fellowship. This group had weathered many storms in the changing landscape of Albanian life and the life of the church and I considered it a privilege to do this.

I no longer had the fluency in the Albanian language which we had both developed whilst living there but I had a wonderful interpreter, Joanna, who made it possible for me to do the job. Joanna became a firm friend and an indispensable part of the team. She was also good at drama and we used improvised sketches to illustrate some of the teaching which we saw as a crucial part of the times with these dear ladies.

During the few months I was there one of the other ladies developed into an excellent assistant and she was more than able to continue the group after we left. Again, we saw that the primary role of foreign 'missionaries' should be to support and encourage native Albanians in leadership positions and then move on. This group prayed, studied God's Word and supported one another in many ways; they also had lots of fun together and many coffees!

The other group was a Bible class, similar to the Kids' clubs we had facilitated in our tiny apartment when we lived there, this time at the orphanage. This was to be on Saturday mornings and was to be aimed at the younger children, around twenty of them. Each week we had a great time with this lively group, teaching them about the love of God as shown in Christ, sharing the gospel and praying with them each week. Once more Dan's practical skills came to the fore as he produced all the resources needed each week, spending many hours on making the worksheets which were just not available locally.

When we left it was marvellous to find out that two of the ladies from my ladies' group, Joanna and her mum, had been approached by Fatos to continue this work and they did so to great effect. Partly developing from this work in the orphanage a group of children has now become part of the Baptist church, and the children's work which we were supposed to set up decades ago has finally been established. Every week we can see the pictures posted on social media of this work and are delighted to know that God is planting seeds in the hearts of many more children and young people in Saranda.

The early summer of 2017 was a wonderful time; we were once more part of the community, if only for a short period, and able to establish work which would continue in our absence. Once more the Jonida Foundation had a lasting impact.

For two more years we and our supporters continued to raise funds and visit several times a year to oversee the progress that each student was making.

As well as this we provided several guitars, which we took over on our trips. (I say we, but it was dear Dan who carried them from airport to boat and beyond!) Mitro, who was an old friend by then and leader of the worship team at the Baptist church, was teaching some of the older boys in the orphanage to play on the only guitar he had. Giving each of these teenagers their own instrument was essential and improved the lessons and their ability to practise. Carrying them over to Albania on our many visits was not easy but Fatos managed to assure the authorities that we were not importing them to sell and they even survived the ‘care’ of the baggage handlers on every flight.

Coffee mornings, concerts, sponsored walks and many other events continued until 2019 when, quite suddenly it seemed, we both felt strongly that the Lord was telling us to wind things up. This came as a bit of a surprise, especially as several other projects with which we were involved also came to a fairly sudden halt. All of our trustees agreed that we should end our involvement in the orphanage although none of us was sure why. Yes, things had improved drastically in the lives of all the children, both materially and in many other ways, but surely this work was still necessary.

Obediently we had to tell our dear friends in Saranda about our decision and in autumn 2019 we travelled over to do this in person. We had bought presents for our teachers and arranged to take them out for coffee, dreading having to tell them the sad news. Amazingly this was not necessary as on our arrival Fatos announced that he would personally take on the funding of these three dear ladies himself. He had become by that time an extremely successful businessman with several prosperous projects including a car hire firm, currency exchange office and local tour business. He really had become the 'Fresh Prince' of Saranda that we had joked about in the early years! We had no doubt that he would carry out his promise and were delighted to just have our annual thank-you meeting with the teachers and wish them well for the future.

So, the work of the Jonida Foundation had come to an end, a little abruptly, along with Dan's work with the local Credit Union community bank in town centre and our private tuition. All of these projects had kept us busy for years and we would miss the many hours of fundraising exploits and especially our involvement in the different projects in Saranda.

Little did we know that not long after our last visit that year it would become impossible for any of this to continue. But of course our amazing God knew what was coming and had, as He always does, prepared the way for us...

16. Covid and Beyond

As I write this latest chapter, I am aware that there are many for whom there was no 'beyond' the Covid pandemic which swept across the globe, and still has an impact upon many lives today. Too many died, so many lost loved ones and today thousands still struggle with the effects of long Covid. The economic future of many nations has been impacted and, as always, the poorest countries are still paying the highest price. In no way am I intending to be glib as I describe our experience of this worldwide catastrophe any more than I intended to minimise the awful repercussions of childhood sexual abuse in the early chapters. Indeed, both of these terrible types of events wreak havoc on the lives of their victims far beyond the immediate damage done by them; not only on their victims but upon the families and communities of which they are a part. Rather, I am hoping to show that in both these and other troubles that we humans are prone to suffer the presence of God in our lives makes a huge difference. From any and all catastrophes He alone can bring healing and restoration.

Covid 19 was, and still is for many, a terrifying prospect which in the early stages was a completely unknown entity and therefore so much more frightening for everyone. As a person still suffering at times from anxiety in daily life and battling at times with the results of past trauma, you would think that the prospect of a sudden and unknown plague creeping across the globe would send me into total panic mode, unable to leave the house and unable to mix with any other human! Of course, as I have learnt, my anxiety is much more likely to result from social pressures and relationship difficulties; stress brought on by having to perform or risk the rejection or even unpleasant reactions of those who I am desperate to be close to, but still longing to allow them to see the real me. The prospect and later reality of 'lockdown' was quite appealing to a person who, although loving people, struggles with the reality of personal interaction. And I know I am not alone.

This was something different, however, and it was a completely natural and understandable anxiety that everyone was experiencing as we waited to see how the plague unfolded. There was some fear in both of us; as asthmatics and a bit older we were both considered to be 'vulnerable' adults who needed to isolate ourselves. The problem was that Dan was an essential worker so this was not going to happen for him, and therefore for me, so we would need to find a way to walk through this minefield with God's help. And, as always, He made a way where there did not seem there was possibly going to be one. He also gave us His word to stand on – yet another promise from my wonderful Father which we both held onto, sometimes literally for dear life, as the storm passed over us and we had to pass through its eye.

Psalm 91 says much about God's protection for us, as does much of His Word, but specifically in this psalm He says three times that He will protect us from plague or pestilence. As the Message puts it:

"His huge, outstretched arms protect you... fear nothing... not disease that prowls through the darkness. Even though others succumb all around you ... no harm will even graze you."

When the first lockdown came Dan was about to go to work, unlike the vast majority of the population, and our dear children were adamant in their advice not to let him go. Even our oldest granddaughter pleaded with him to stay home and only when we asked them that if he was a doctor would they say the same did they relent. He was an essential worker and as such needed to put himself on the front line. He, our wonderful firefighter son and amazing schools' worker daughter all did this throughout the worst of the pandemic and we had to trust God for them all.

To say that this was hard is a massive understatement but we had no choice. Every day when I drove him to work (there were no buses of course) I knew that he could be bringing the virus home with him. No masks, no vaccine, no protection at all except the hand of God. But this is the hand of God, Creator, Redeemer, Provider, Protector, Healer and so much more.

Each night he would come home, walking the two and a half miles to protect me from infection, taking off all his work clothes in the porch and showering before he came into the main house. We slept in separate rooms for weeks and tried to socially distance at home; that final precaution lasted about three days!

And we prayed! For our lives, our family and our friends. For the NHS, those who were sick or had lost loved ones and for the Government as they steered us through this. Most of all we prayed for our nation that the people of this land would wake up to their desperate need for Salvation; for that spiritual awakening that we had longed to see here in England, in the islands of the UK; in our institutions, our population, in our precious family and of course in the Church. That we, God's people,might wake up to the state of our own lives and that of the people around us.

Slowly but steadily we began to grow in faith and this was in great part helped by the wonderful fellowship to which the Lord had moved us only the summer before the virus hit these shores. Riverside Church has become our spiritual home, the people there our church family, but in late 2019 we had only just begun our journey with them. Despite this we were loved, accepted, encouraged, comforted and strengthened by this amazing fellowship of believers.

'Online meetings' was not a thing for us pre-Covid but it soon became less of 'online' and more of a 'lifeline'. Each week we 'met' with our Sunday morning prayer group, 'Zoom' was added to our vocabulary for the first time, and later we tuned in on YouTube to the Sunday morning service, which lasted right up to the wonderful time when we could meet 'in real life' (another new phrase to add to our everyday speech!) There was even virtual 'homegroup' in our own homes where small group meetings could continue live for all who could tune in.

There were going to be those who could not access all of these or whose relationship with technology meant that they just would not, but many hundreds, if not thousands, across the nations met as 'Church' like this for months. My friend from the Philippines met with her home church because the fellowship she attended in England had no online services. She still 'meets' with them today!

We were so cared for by our Heavenly Father, protected, provided for and even given tremendous opportunities to see and speak with family across the miles, again through Zoom and WhatsApp. It was as if all of this technology had been developed for such a time as this and we continue to make so much more use of it even now when it is not crucial to keep our distance.

Once more our amazing God made a way where there seemed to be no way. The shape of Church may have changed but the love, fellowship, care and empowerment has not. Whenever and wherever we worship the Lord we join the host of Heaven and all the saints who are always praising and adoring our wonderful Saviour, so none of these restrictions hampered our ability to transcend the natural, imperfect and now downright precarious world around us and enter those Heavenly places. Moreover, it gave us a much clearer insight into the lives of our brothers and sisters in countries where there is real persecution of Christians and so many live in fear of imprisonment or even death all the time. Many parts of the Church always meet in secret, if they can meet at all. Many cannot even use social media platforms because of government surveillance and the danger discovery brings.

The vaccine became available – a miracle really in the timescale available – and everywhere we went there were masks and people keeping their distance. This was especially hard for grandchildren to understand and made sleepovers impossible. We missed the closeness which this brought with these precious ones, we missed trips to the children's homes generally and we did not see Isaac, except on video calls, for over five years. His home in the USA was always a distance away but Covid made it too far to travel for his usual two-yearly trip.

Eventually life went back to normal, the new normal as we called it, with many people still working from home and many more video meetings than before, both for work and family chats. We had a series of vaccines and did not succumb to the virus until after the third one, only having a fairly mild bout of flu-like symptoms. Once more the Lord had been good for His word, He protected us and we survived and indeed prospered. Not only us but also our children and grandchildren all came through it unscathed, despite some of them having Covid; all fully recovered and the Lord continues to bless them and keep them in His care.

17. The End?

A little over 45 years ago I began this wonderful adventure with Jesus. That amazing night, in the middle of the night, when I first became aware that God was real and that He had something to say to me, little did I know that this was going to be the most amazing, life-changing experience it was possible for any human to have. All I needed to do was to hold on tight and it was going to be the ride of my life, of anyone's life, and it has been! Holding on tight to the Lord has not always been easy and there have been days when I nearly let go, but He has never let go of me. He never will let go of those who have really given their lives to Him. Not only that but He has a plan for our lives, for those who are following Him, just like He did for those first followers two thousand years ago in Judea.

At the start of this story, my story, I sat at my dining table surrounded by photographs of my wonderful family. Christmas had just gone and another crop of these were part of our presents as usual, including the obligatory school photos. Wonderful! Above my table now are lovely photos of the six grandchildren taken at family gatherings over the years showing their growth and closeness.

Once again, I marvel at the grace of my loving heavenly Father. This is because I am aware, more than any of the happy smiling faces who look down on me while I write, that without Him I could never have received this amazing inheritance. Four children, their spouses, six grandchildren, our baby great granddaughter, and my lovely husband Dan surround me with love and blessings every day of my life. This was all I ever wanted, all my life, to be part of a loving family. God has done this and it is amazing.

Only He could have taken the 'sow's ear' that was the mess of my mangled and dysfunctional life and transform it into the 'silk purse' I now enjoy. Without Him I was incapable of building the successful, happy, caring human relationships which are so necessary for the creation of loving families and communities. Without Him I really doubt that I would still be here today decades later to celebrate His glorious gifts and witness to His restoration.

My friends and family have no idea who I was and how far I have travelled to be the person I am now – still an unfinished article but so very different from the woman I would have been without His work in my life.

In 1978, at the age of 27, God rescued me from the life I had and I wrote a new song. It begins with what has become the story of this life, of any life fully committed to Him:

"Peace, peace is flowing like a river from Your throne

And Peace, peace is growing in my heart and therefore in my home

I can see Jesus changing me, I can see Jesus arranging me

Into the woman He wants me to be

Into the person He made me to be

Jesus is changing me."

When I gave my life to Christ, began to trust Him for my future, believing that I was forgiven and could spend my life both on this Earth and forever living in His love, I had no idea what that meant. One thing I did know was that I was a mess. My choices had spoilt my life and the life of those closest to me; the poison that had been infecting my soul from early childhood was eventually going to destroy me and

I had no way of escaping the person I had become. My inability to love my baby boy the way I wanted to do had brought this all to a head and it was this new and fairly dysfunctional role as a mother which made me so open to the revelation that God had in store. In addition, I knew that I had done some very wrong things, as I think everyone does, but, like most people, I had buried this knowledge deeply in my subconscious and done my best to forget them. Guilt is a slow-burning fuse, a destructive tumour that eventually causes us to falter and fail in so many areas of our lives.

When I realised that Jesus had forgiven me, would go on doing so even when I got it wrong and was never going to leave or reject me, I began to respond with a love which I had never been able to feel or express before; a love which I had never experienced or been capable of before. This love came from Him, Heavenly love which we can only fully know when we know the King of kings.

It poured out of me in song and service to my King. I just wanted to serve Him even though I did not know how to or could even do a very good job. Like the woman in Luke's account of Jesus's life in chapter seven of his description of those amazing days around 2,000 years ago, I was that 'fallen woman' who knew that she was a sinner, knew that she was a complete failure and had lost any sense of a moral compass. She poured tears over His feet and dried them with her hair because she knew that she was forgiven and accepted by her Saviour. She knew that He, Jesus, was God because only God could take away her sense of shame and guilt and make her feel accepted and loved. I too now knew this.

What I did not know was that this same Jesus was going to take my broken life and show me not only forgiveness but mercy, grace, acceptance and belonging.

His complete love. Not only had He wiped my slate clean, even though I did not understand or fully appreciate this, I knew that this was true and much, much more.

I always say that I am a slow learner but maybe God is just taking His time with me as He always treats us as the unique individual that He created us to be. The truth is that in that 45 years I know Jesus has been changing not only me but every relationship in which I find myself.

As John Donne, many years ago the Dean of St Paul's Cathedral, said:

'No man is an island entire of itself; every man is a piece of the continent, a part of the main; Any man's death diminishes me, because I am involved in mankind.....'

In his poem he shows how we all are interlinked, relational beings, whose lives all affect one another. Each one of us is like part of a continent that, if broken off, lessens the whole.In every sense our lives are connected to the lives of those around us whether those closest to us or those on the other side of the planet. More than this I know that our lives have a very direct effect on those nearest to us. From my catastrophic childhood relationships, which helped to sadly mould me in the wrong way, to the wonderful love of my children and grandchildren and of course the loving care which Dan has showered on me since our earliest times. The way we treat each other matters. From the daily routines of family life to the way nations treat nations, relationships matter. This is why the Lord spoke so often of the Kingdom of God, a sphere in which love is pre-eminent and He is central in all our relationships, in all of our life. The Church, (those who love and follow our risen Jesus not the man-made structures and traditions of religious Christendom), is our spiritual family where we grow and help each other to grow more like Him every day. This is why He taught us to pray 'Our Father' because we have a family of God where we grow and learn to worship Him with our whole life, together.

Proverbs, the amazing wisdom book which Dan and I are studying at the moment, says:

"With his mouth the Godless destroys his neighbour,

But through knowledge the righteous escape.

When the righteous prosper the city rejoices;

When the wicked perish, there are shouts of joy.

Through the blessing of the upright a city is exalted,

But by the mouth of the wicked it is destroyed."

Proverbs 11 vs 9 - 11

Who we are, how we live, the way we treat others and care for our communities, affects everything and everyone around us. Like ripples on a lake the 'stone' of our life lands in time and space and sends out influences all around. We have social media 'influencers' now apparently who are followed and emulated by millions but little do we realise that we are all influencers. From the smile that is shared with a neighbour on their lowest day to the angry comment we make in the supermarket when our brand of peas is not in stock! From the broken family relationship which damages the lives of all those involved to the terrible invasion of a neighbouring country which leads to destroyed infrastructure and terrible loss of lives. Our actions matter.

As Jesus began to transform my emotionally scarred, mentally warped existence, He also changed the way I related to others. The very first example was only hours after meeting Him when I realised that my tiny baby boy no longer screamed every time I picked him up. Isaac became much more settled and content, sensing that I was now able to feel the wonder of all wonders – maternal love. This was a new sensation for me, having someone whose life was so much more precious than anything else and whose welfare was my only concern. Love, real love, for the first time in my life caring more for his welfare than my own. Before this I was extremely self-centred and calculating. Many times before this I would manipulate people and situations so that I could get my own way, the only way that I would feel safe. In my paranoid existence the constant fear made me very insecure and a complete control freak.

For many years I had used alcohol as a crutch and would often drink until reality was fuzzy in order to cope with the fear and self-hatred which sometimes had nearly overwhelmed me. Now I began to learn that in order to 'love my neighbour as myself' I had to first learn how to stop hating myself and this was going to be a long process. Much of the healing came through forgiveness. Knowing that our shame is washed away also eradicates self-loathing. The real freedom that Jesus brings through His forgiving love allows us to live in that freedom, and shows us how to forgive others. All those who had abused me had to have my forgiveness in order for me to be really free. As I experienced that day a few years ago when I knew my abuser had no longer any power over me, that I had forgiven him, I allowed the grace of God to bring real release from those hobnail footprints which had damaged my heart all those years ago,

If we can see ourselves as Jesus sees us, reflected in the love which took Him to that awful cross to die for us, we begin to see our value and in fact love ourselves however much that reflection has been distorted. But it takes time. I, and my children, had to go through so much pain to eventually experience the changes necessary. Of course, seeing them suffer was terrible and was my responsibility in part, but I know that they have been covered by His great love and blessings too and marvel at the lovely people that they have become. One day they will, I am now sure, realise Who it is who has been with them all through their lives and turn once more to Him as they did as children. For many years now Dan and I have prayed for them, and their children, that they would turn and recognise that Jesus is real and their Saviour. As young children they all had a childlike faith but walked away over the years and only the Lord knows what they really believe now. At times this has made me anxious that they will not be safe when Jesus returns or they leave this Earth.

Quite recently though, through the prayers of an old friend in the church, God showed me that He has never left them and then He spoke to me as clearly as only He can, just this year.

I was walking by the river in late August and the tree-lined path up to the cherry orchard was dark and shady for the most part but it was speckled with dapples of light here and there. Sometimes there was a fork in the road where the light shone brightly onto one path but was much darker on the other fork. Each path eventually led to open fields flooded with late summer sunshine and stretching as far as the eye could see.

And God spoke to me in that clear, quiet, inner voice of calm:

'The path is their lives, those who we love and pray for daily. The darkness is the way that many of them have chosen to live, away from the Lord. The dappled areas are where the light of Christ breaks through as He reaches out to them and blesses, protects, heals and positively directs them. As you pray for them His love reaches out to them and touches their lives even when you cannot.

'The light path, where the road forks, is where they have had opportunities to walk back to Christ's presence but chose not to do so (rather like me at seventeen).

'The land around the paths which is flooded with light is where I am, says the Lord, where one day according to My promise they will eventually be reconciled to me, trusting in My salvation. Then they will know My presence for all eternity – walking in the light at last and living for My Glory.'

As I write this, with tears in my eyes, I no longer despair, but still long for that time. It may be when I have left this Earth but it will almost certainly be after I publish this book. The important thing is that I now believe that it will be, learning to give more and more of my fears to Him as He ever works on my faith which must grow if I am to be all that He has planned for me to be.

Just as when I began this story, Christmas has just passed once more, the best one so far; every Christmas is better than the one before in the Kingdom of my King. We have the usual crop of photographs, this time on social media for the most part and including for the first time our first (of many we trust) great grandchild. We look forward to the coming year with faith and trust in the one who has already seen the future and holds us in His hands.

Over the years since the first few weeks of this wonderful new life in Christ there have been many, many changes but He has always been the constant and faithful presence that He promised to be. He has never failed us and as we start this new year He will not fail us now. My darling Dan has a new catchphrase, which he lovingly encourages me with whatever each new day brings: 'Life is an adventure', and so with God's help I am going to embrace whatever life brings, enjoying this amazing adventure with the love of my life and our Lord.

The great Charles H Spurgeon once said these wise words and we will attempt to continue the great adventure of all the saints of God while we still live on this planet with this faith:

'My faith rests not in what I am, or shall be, or feel, or know but in what Christ is, in what He has done and what He is now doing for me.'